THE
LINUX
SOLUTION

[HOW TO BUILD AND SUPPORT
SCALABLE IT SYSTEMS
USING THE POWER OF LINUX]

KEITH EDMUNDS

RƎTHINK PRESS

First published in Great Britain 2019
by Rethink Press (www.rethinkpress.com)
© Copyright Keith Edmunds

All proceeds from this book will be donated to Great Ormond Street Children's Hospital Charity.

Thank you GOSH: you do an amazing job.

Contents

Introduction

This book is a practical guide to building and maintaining an IT infrastructure using Linux. No matter whether you intend to carry out that work in-house, or outsource some or all of it, this book will guide you through defining your requirements, implementing the systems, supporting them on a day-to-day basis and reviewing the entire process. Before we get into the detail, I'm going to tell you a little about myself. After that, the rest of the book is about building and maintaining the best Linux solution for your business.

Born right at the tail end of the 1950s, I had a child's natural curiosity. My parents were frustrated by the fact that, with every Christmas and birthday, each new toy would be taken apart to see how it worked before being reassembled. They partially cured that by buying me a Meccano set for my seventh birthday, thus forcing me to build my own toys rather than take manufactured ones apart. Neat move.

After leaving school, I spent the first four years working for (as it was called in those days) the General Post Office, or GPO. Despite the name, my job was isolating problems with international telephone calls (or 'finding out why it didn't work'). Later this part of the GPO became what we now know as British Telecom. Back then, no one seemed to care how much or how little I worked, so there was little incentive to excel. I thought I could do better, so I looked around and noticed that the computer industry seemed to be coming to the fore. I'd already started a computer club back at school (despite us having no computers), and I thought it would be amazing if I could now work with real computers. I found a job with Digital Equipment Corporation, a large American computer company, and quit the GPO.

The first lesson: Don't waste your time in a job you hate. It was 1980, and I was twenty-one years old.

I started with Digital in November 1980. I can remember the first day quite clearly, and boy was it different from the GPO. At 08:45 the office was buzzing, people charging around, phones ringing, people rushing in, people rushing out. I was in the midst of a seemingly chaotic yet also dynamic office, and it was great. My job title was 'Terminal Specialist', which seemed to have sinister overtones, but in reality I spent my time fixing computer terminals. Anyone much younger than I am will probably have little idea of what I am talking about, but these were dumb terminals that spoke down a wire to the Big Computer in the Computer Room somewhere. I had a van full of parts, and I would drive from one customer to the next and fix their broken terminals. That gave me time with customers, which I loved, and time fixing things, which I also loved. I was having the time of my life, and I was getting paid for it. Six months after starting I had the 'job plan and review' meeting with my manager. Things were going well, and I was looking forward to the meeting. We sat down, and after the small talk he asked me what my job was. Somewhat surprised (shouldn't he know already?), I said, 'Fixing computer terminals.' 'No,' was his reply, 'it's fixing customers.' That was nearly forty years ago, but it sticks in my mind. He was right, too.

Lesson number two: Fix the customer.

The computer industry during the 1980s was rocketing. Digital was growing at a rate of 40% per year, and it was a very inspirational place to work. I learned a lot – not only about computing, but also about myself – and I started to change from an effervescent, lively and somewhat naive young man into a slightly more mature character. I'd moved on to fixing bigger things than computer terminals by now; I was fixing 'proper' computers. In those days they really were big: six feet tall and often as wide, if not wider.

I had calmed down a little too: I recall visiting the IT department of a big off-licence where there had recently been too many problems with the computer system. I was in the IT manager's office – a really nice guy who always made sure the computer engineers had a little bottle of something for Christmas – but today he was unhappy. Not unreasonably, because he'd had more than his fair share of computing problems in the previous few weeks. He told me how bad it had been, how people weren't competent at fixing things, and more besides. I remember thinking, 'It's broken right now, and every minute I spend sitting here is another minute your system is down' – but of course my job was to fix the customer. I listened, we talked, we stopped, I fixed it, we got on fine.

Lesson number three: Take the time to listen to the customer.

Towards the end of the 1980s, the computing industry finished its flirtation with high growth and big revenues, and more than a few of my friends changed jobs, companies and, in some cases, careers. In the early 1990s, I too took a redundancy package, and I joined a small software distribution company which, at the time, consisted of ten people. This was

very different from the large international corporation that I had left, but it was also great fun. In some
ways it reminded me of how Digital had been in the
1980s: fast-paced, frenetic and full of the belief that
we could do almost anything. What was interesting in this new business was that the MD, who had
built the company up from scratch, seemed to find
it very hard to delegate without constantly looking
over the delegatee's shoulder. I understand why, but
it restricted the growth of his company.

Lesson number four: Grow yourself with the
business.

Meanwhile, and also in the early 1990s – on 25
August 1991, to be precise – a young Internet was hit
with sixty-one words that would change the course
of IT history:

I'm doing a (free) operating system (just a
hobby, won't be big and professional like gnu)
for 386(486) AT clones. This has been brewing
since april, and is starting to get ready. I'd like
any feedback on things people like/dislike in
minix, as my OS resembles it somewhat (same
physical layout of the file-system (due to practical
reasons) among other things).

Those words were written by Linus Torvalds,
a twenty-one-year-old Finnish student at the

University of Helsinki, and led to what we now call Linux.

That posting had a profound impact on the world of commercial computing from both a technical and a philosophical perspective. Technically, a new operating system was introduced; philosophically, the concept of Open Source software gained visibility.

Today, Linux in one form or another is in widespread use. It's used in TV set-top boxes, central heating controllers, cars, mobile phones and on the International Space Station. It is what powers Google, Amazon and Wikipedia, and as of November 2017, every one of the world's top 500 supercomputers runs Linux. On top of all of that, there are millions of businesses all over the world, from one-man bands to international corporations, that rely on Linux.

Working in the IT industry in a technical role as I was, I had become aware of Linux early on. It was new, and it was exciting. Now I could see how the operating system worked. I could take it apart, play with it, even break it without having to confess to my parents.

One thing led to another, as happens, and these days I'm the CEO of Tiger Computing, an IT Solutions business based in the beautiful Wye Valley on the England–Wales border. Tiger Computing started as a Linux support and consultancy business in 2002, and since then we've worked with a variety of clients across all industries with a notable bias towards high-tech engineering, bioscience and businesses with larger IT infrastructures.

Linux is free, both in the sense of there being no charge for the license and in the sense of it being unrestricted. The French talk of *gratis* and *libre*, respectively; the English talk of 'Free as in beer' and 'Free as in speech', which tells you about the cultural differences between the English and the French as well as their sense of humour.

Businesses are drawn to Linux for a variety of reasons. The price point is undoubtedly an attraction for some, but for others the flexibility, interoperability, security and wide range of applications are more important.

The fact that Linux is free doesn't mean it's easy to work with. Not every business has the great experience with Linux that they hoped for. For some, ensuring that the infrastructure is able to meet the evolving needs of the business is their concern. For others, there are nagging doubts: Are our systems secure? Can I improve reliability? For some, interruptions to their real job to answer a Linux issue is a real problem. There is a limit to how much time you can afford or want to spend being a Linux administrator when that's not actually your job. If we're not careful, fire-fighting becomes the norm. Even when the issues are resolved, there's a nagging doubt that they may not stay resolved.

The businesses Tiger Computing worked with employed some very smart people, but although they often had a good understanding of technology, we increasingly found that the interrelationship between the various systems was lacking. We'd see businesses with multiple systems, each of which would work well in isolation but which caused conflict when they tried to work together. We'd see complex and error-prone processes created to try to work around deficiencies in the underlying infrastructure. We'd see employees and management alike getting frustrated that things didn't 'just work'.

What was often missing was infrastructure design. A lot of these businesses were Venture Capitalist backed, and there was pressure from day one to get something – almost anything – in place. As the businesses tasted success and grew, the underlying infrastructure lacked robustness, but the pressure was on to grow more, to deliver more. The result was an IT infrastructure that slowly, day by day, became less and less fit for purpose.

Over the years at Tiger Computing, we've developed and refined a methodology that has helped businesses like that turn the corner. They have secure, resilient and scalable infrastructures that support the business needs. Their staff are able to focus on their chosen careers rather than being sidelined into fire-fighting IT problems. IT has become a tool they just use, rather than an irritating distraction. Everything works.

The focus from businesses has evolved, too. Once the demand was specifically for Linux. That still exists, of course, but businesses today are less interested in how it works ('It runs on Linux'). They are much more interested in how well it enables them to achieve specific outcomes ('Can it do this, worldwide, in a secure, resilient and scalable way?'). Google, Amazon, Wikipedia, Salesforce, Facebook: they all run on Linux, but the focus is rightly on the applications.

My colleagues at Tiger Computing and I have contributed to various Open Source projects over the years, and now I want to share our way of building robust IT infrastructures. It was only once I started writing this book that I realised that there was a pattern. All of my life I have been curious about how things work, understanding the detail and improving things where I can. I've also always wanted to explain how things work, right from when I was a cadet in the Air Training Corps, through running technical training courses, to how I spend my weekends these days, teaching people to fly gliders. This book is more of the same: I'm passionate about what we do at Tiger Computing, and I want to share that with you.

This book describes the methodology we use. I'll highlight the most common problems and how to avoid them, and I'll help you draw up a strategy that will ensure you get maximum value from your IT infrastructure.

There are four steps to the methodology, and this book is split into four corresponding sections:

- **R**equirements: The first step is to clearly define, in writing, what the end result must deliver and how it will fit into any existing infrastructure. It's here that we define some essential business criteria around Service Level Agreements, backups, security and more. Skip this foundation step and the mistakes will be both plentiful and expensive – and until the requirements are defined, mistakes will keep being made.

- **I**mplementation: Once the requirements are defined, design and build a robust infrastructure that can meet those requirements. This is the most technical section of the book. If you don't have in-depth technical staff, you may need some assistance with implementation, but this section provides an overview of technologies available, techniques to consider and questions to ask.

- **S**upport: The processes, procedures and tools that manage the day-to-day operations necessary to keep your infrastructure safe, secure and available. Keeping systems running seamlessly day to day is a bit like juggling: it looks easy when someone competent does it, but it's a bit trickier than it looks. I'll pull back the covers and show you what a smart support operation looks like, how it works and what it needs to be successful. This is an area commonly outsourced, and there's some advice about how to go about doing that in Chapter 22.

- **E**valuate: Neither technology nor your business remain static. As each evolves, you need to review and update the Requirements, Implementation and Support processes accordingly. You also need to test whether your infrastructure works, or can be recovered, under adverse conditions. We'll look at how to test that.

That's the RISE methodology. Three out of four isn't enough: you need all four steps. When one or more is missing, you'll have problems. You end up wasting a lot of time and money, you risk losing or damaging your intellectual property, but most of all you risk your key people getting frustrated and simply jumping ship.

When all four steps are in place, you have a secure, scalable and resilient infrastructure. Building and maintaining such an infrastructure requires a systematic approach. Over many years of working with clients who bet their businesses on Linux, we've used and refined our methodology, and it works. It scales from one or two Linux systems to thousands.

From time to time throughout this book I'll refer you to a *Resources* web page, and that may be found at www.tiger-computing.co.uk/the-linux-solution.

The first section, Requirements, is just over the page. Shall we get started?

SECTION ONE

REQUIREMENTS

CHAPTER ONE

Why Write Requirements?

Why is it that some businesses seem to have a Linux infrastructure that just works, with users able to do the tasks they want to be doing without distractions, whereas other businesses always seem to have just one more niggling issue to sort out before 'everything will be fine'? The difference is often that the former have taken the time to define their requirements, whereas the latter are sure they know what they are doing but haven't thought it through, let alone written it down.

A Requirements Document defines what you are trying to achieve. Businesses that don't have defined, written Requirements Documents find that they spend too much time bending their Linux infrastructure to meet their (undefined) needs: systems are unreliable and are used inefficiently; storage space is not available where it is needed; too many people are involved in day-to-day IT drudge work; unexpected expenses occur too often. By contrast, businesses that do have defined, written Requirements Documents make good use of their IT resources, and, on the whole, IT becomes a 'solved problem' for them, meeting the evolving needs of the business and freeing staff to do the work they want to be doing.

A key aspect of a successful Requirements Document is that it must focus on *what* must be achieved and completely ignore *how* it may be achieved. One common mistake is muddying the waters with implementation details. It's all too easy to couch the requirements such that they lead towards a (possibly unconsciously chosen) specific solution. A real-world example is, 'Two servers will be needed for redundancy'. What is the requirement here? It is almost certainly *not* that two servers be used, regardless. This requirement says nothing about the relationship between the two servers (will one be kept in a box on the shelf 'just in case'?). Question the requirements with 'why', and keep doing that until you unearth the real requirement:

'Two servers will be needed for redundancy.'

'Why?'

'Because we don't want a single point of failure.'

'Why?'

'Because for every minute the server is down, we lose £1,000.'

'So is the requirement, "Better than 99.99% availability"?'

'Oh. Yes.'

'Is that availability of the server, or of the service it provides?'

'Ah. Good question…'

The Requirements Document must be in writing. It doesn't need to be a huge document, but putting things in writing increases clarity and reduces ambiguity, both enviable attributes. The content of the Requirements Document will vary from business to business, but the chapter titles in this section will serve you well as a starting point.

The Requirements Document serves a number of purposes:

- It clarifies thought. Just thinking through the points will lead to a more refined, more appropriate infrastructure.

- It gives consistency. By defining all the requirements at the outset, you can ensure that they do not conflict with one another. Far easier to resolve such conflicts before we start implementing.

- It becomes a checklist. Once your Linux infrastructure is up and running, reviewing the requirements will show whether you really do have everything in place.

- It allows your infrastructure to evolve. Over time, requirements change. Identifying the change within your Requirements Document makes it easier to determine what needs to change within the infrastructure.

- It brings consensus. Agreeing requirements means that everyone involved, both within the business and externally, is aiming for the same result.

There are multiple potential audiences for your Requirements Document. They will include:

- **Business Managers.** They are (usually) responsible for ensuring that the business is profitable. The Linux infrastructure is a business asset: it has a cost associated, and it should deliver some benefit that outweighs the cost. It's appropriate that the business managers agree what that infrastructure should deliver.

- **Users.** One would like to think that the users' requirements would be similar to those of the business managers, but often users will see a greater level of detail. Their requirements will commonly stem from perceived shortcomings in existing or previous systems they have used. 'I don't want to have to copy data from one system to another to do my job' is a reasonable requirement, but the business managers may not even know that that's going on.

- **Technical Staff.** Those who will be designing your infrastructure will naturally need to understand the goals of the system, and it's helpful for those who will be supporting it to understand its purpose too. The level of detail needed for each group will be different, but having one definitive place to go to find out what the business is trying to achieve is helpful for everyone.

The Requirements Document may refer to or encompass other documents. In particular, there may be a separate Security Policy and an Acceptable Use Policy, both discussed in Chapter 4.

Throughout this section we will use a fictitious company, Super Consulting Ltd, as an example of how a Requirements Document might be developed. Super Consulting Ltd is a business consultancy working on projects with various clients. This company has developed a proprietary tool, its Business Analysis Tool (BAT), which is key to how it conducts business.

The starting point of the Requirements Document is a single paragraph at the beginning that summarises the overall purpose of the Linux infrastructure. This isn't about detail; rather, it's there to give someone who is unfamiliar with your business some context to start from.

Examples:

- The purpose of the Linux infrastructure is to manage code development, including debugging, validation testing and documentation, for the new range of audio processing chips being developed

- The purpose of the Linux infrastructure is to host our clients' websites and facilitate online payments

Here's the summary paragraph for Super Consulting Ltd:

The purpose of the Linux infrastructure is to analyse clients' businesses, and manage and track client projects, workload and billing.

SUMMARY

- The Requirements Document brings clarity, consistency and consensus

- It must focus on *what* is to be achieved, not *how* it will be achieved

- It should be agreed by all parties before implementation begins

Over the past fifteen-plus years, the biggest single mistake we've seen with some of our clients at Tiger Computing has been the lack of defined requirements. It leads to wasted money and wasted time, and the irony is that at *some* point the requirements have to be defined anyway, even if only by trial and error. When the department head wants one thing and the research scientists want another, the time to resolve that conflict is before any buying decisions are made.

The difference that having a Requirements Document makes is huge, but writing an effective one is deceptively hard. It feels as if it should be simple, straightforward, obvious even; but, like the onion, there are multiple layers and there's more to it than initially meets the eye.

Now that we have our summary paragraph, we'd better add some detail.

CHAPTER TWO

Requirements For Day-To-Day Operations

In an ideal world, our systems would be available 24/7. In reality, that's seldom the case. In order to ensure we build an infrastructure that's fit for purpose, we need to define what our availability requirements are.

The starting point is to consider what the non-availability of a service costs your business. It's likely that this varies by time of day and day of the week, and possibly by time of year. Which services are the most critical to the business? Unplanned outages, by definition, can occur at any time, so budget for them occurring at the worst time. Conversely, what are the best times for planned maintenance that may include service unavailability?

Our Requirements Document should list the normal hours of operation, the response required to resolve issues during and outside those times, and when scheduled downtime is acceptable (if ever). How might our fictitious business, Super Consulting Ltd, handle this? Its analysis found that:

- Core business hours are 08:00 to 18:00, Monday to Friday. System availability outside of those times is far less critical.

- Mondays were slightly more critical than the rest of the week as that was when planning meetings took place.

- Within the 08:00–18:00 window, after 15:00 was less critical, and Friday afternoons were the least critical of all core hours.

- Requirements were constant throughout the year.

- The project management system was the most business-critical system.

- A four-hour outage of the project management system on a Monday morning would be very unwelcome, but its impact to the business could be contained.

IT people sometimes talk of 'resilience', by which they mean 'availability of a service', particularly under adverse conditions (eg, hardware failure). A service might be email, a website, a code repository, and so on. Our focus should be on the availability required of the service itself rather than the availability of any one server or system that provides it. How resilience is achieved is an implementation issue; from a requirements perspective, so long as the website is up and running correctly, we don't care that one or other of the systems involved in providing that service has a problem.

With respect to planned maintenance, one phrase the IT industry likes is 'at risk'. During 'at risk' time, no downtime is expected but there is an increased risk of it occurring. For example, a server may have two independent power feeds. If one needs to be disconnected to perform maintenance, the service is said to be 'at risk' because now if the remaining feed fails, the service itself will become unavailable.

Here are Super Consulting's availability requirements:

- Services must generally be available 08:00–18:00

- 'At risk' work may be performed by prior agreement after 16:00 on a weekday

- More extensive planned maintenance must take place outside core business hours or after 15:00 on Fridays

- Target: no more than one unplanned service outage exceeding four hours per year during core business hours

The response times required are:

Severity	Example	Response Time (within core hours)	Response Time (outside core hours)
Critical	A key service has failed or degraded, affecting 5 or more users, and no workaround is available.	10 minutes	1 hour
Serious	A key service has failed or degraded, affecting fewer than 5 users, and no workaround is available.	1 hour	4 hours
Moderate	A non-key service has failed or degraded, affecting 5 or more users, and no workaround is available.	4 hours	Next working day
Minor	Either: (i) a workaround is available for a service failure or degradation as described above; or (ii) a non-key service has failed or degraded, affecting fewer than 5 users.	8 hours	Next working day

SERVICE LEVEL AGREEMENTS

Some providers have Service Level Agreements (SLAs) worded in terms of 'percentage uptime'. For businesses that do not have consistent availability requirements 24/7, this is deceptive. In the example above, Super Consulting Ltd is allowing for four hours' downtime per year, which means the system must be available for 8,756 of the 8,760 hours in a year. That's 99.95% uptime: a laudable goal but probably unnecessary because it treats all 8,760 hours of the year as equal. The actual requirement specifies 'during core business hours'. Those hours are 08:00–18:00, Monday to Friday, so that's a target of around 99.8% – but the impact of that 0.2% downtime varies greatly according to when it occurs.

Some providers offer guaranteed 100% uptime. That's unachievable: such a claim is a marketing headline rather than a factual one. The guarantee, of course, is only about compensation. A typical compensation, payable for up to three hours' unavailability in a month, is 3% of the monthly fee. That is unlikely to represent the cost of the downtime to your business.

SLAs and uptime claims may have a role to play, but the reputation of the provider should also be taken into account.

PRODUCTION, TESTING AND DEVELOPMENT SYSTEMS

All of the preceding points relate to production systems: those that are either revenue generating or which directly support activities that are revenue generating. For some businesses, that will represent all of their systems, but for others there will be development or test systems, the latter sometimes known as User Acceptance Testing (UAT) systems.

There is seldom a need for the development and UAT systems to have the same level of availability as production systems; for example, it's rare that either are needed outside of core business hours. It's worth considering what availability these systems might require, and documenting that in the Requirements Document.

A further consideration is the versions of system software that are installed on non-production systems. For the most part, you want them to be identical to the versions on the production systems – after all, the software being developed or tested will presumably move to the production systems at some point. However, both development and UAT systems can be used to test compatibility with upcoming changes to system software; for example, if a new major release of your chosen Linux distribution is coming out, you may want to test it before rolling it out to production. Under such circumstances, your development and UAT systems may differ from production ones. You should consider how you want to manage that difference and ensure that any divergence between production and UAT/development is understood.

Here's how Super Consulting Ltd defined that requirement:

- Development and test systems must be available 08:00–18:00, Monday to Friday
- Serious or critical issues must be resolved within four hours; moderate or minor issues within one working day
- It must take less than four hours to rebuild any development or test machine to replicate the software environment used in production

---

SUMMARY

- Define the availability required both during and outside of core business hours

- Consider the availability requirements of any development or test systems

- Manage how development and test systems will be a realistic representation of the production environment

For the most part, this section of the Requirements Document defines what 'normal' looks like. It doesn't guarantee availability of systems – that's largely impossible – but it sets expectations. Of all the sections in the Requirements Document, this is the most crucial one for all parties to buy into.

CHAPTER THREE

Backup Requirements

Just about every IT service is comprised of three elements: data, an application that can manipulate and present that data, and hardware to run the application on. As a simple example: a word-processing document represents the data, your word-processing program manipulates and presents that data to you, and it all runs on your desktop PC. Thus, in order to make a service available, we need all three elements – the data, the program and some hardware – available. These elements are listed in order of decreasing criticality: your document is unique, so you *must* have your data. The word-processing program can be the one you have or the one your colleague uses (they may not even be the same program), and, lastly, almost any PC will do. The data, though, is critical.

We discussed availability of systems and services in the previous chapter, but sometimes either a human error or a hardware failure can lead to the data being unavailable. Under such circumstances, we look to backups to restore that data, and within the Requirements Document we need to define the backup criteria.

DATA TYPES

It's easy to say, 'All data must be backed up remotely every night', but that's neither practical nor necessary. All data is not equal, and may be categorised under one of the following headings:

Static data is data that never changes. Some examples:

- Reference data, often from an external source

- The executable programs that are run

- The files from that project that was completed last August

Users need access to this data, but they will never be changing it.

Ephemeral data is data that is transient in nature. It has a short lifespan and is easily, cheaply and often automatically regenerated if needed. Examples tend to be somewhat technical in nature, and include:

- Cached data for a website

- The local copy of a central code repository

- The intermediate files generated when compiling code, such as logs and object files

Business-critical data is data that, if unavailable, would threaten the survival of the business. This is likely to be a very small subset of the overall data, and often comprises the business's intellectual property. Examples include:

- The contents of a source code repository

- The database and code comprising customer websites

- The detailed methodologies used by a consulting company

Business-operational data is used to manage the business day to day, and comprises the likes of client lists, calendars, accounts, proposals, and so on. If lost, the business would undoubtedly lose efficiency, and it may well lose money or even a client or two. However, the business would probably survive.

Normal data is all other data. This is data that, if unavailable, would be irritating, annoying or inconvenient, but would not have a major impact upon the day-to-day operation of the business.

Identifying the category that each element of data falls into is necessary because our requirements for the availability of each category may be different. If you ask your staff what data is business-critical, a common answer would be 'all of it'. That's an understandable perspective: if some data that they had identified as not being business-critical is lost and there's no backup, they may well feel that they will be blamed. So what are the backup requirements for each type of data?

For static data, we need a backup but we don't need to refresh that backup. One or two copies are fine. In some cases – for example, reference data from a manufacturer – we can obtain another copy relatively easily, so we may not need a backup at all. In other cases, we may have an archive of the data and keep a local copy for reference.

Ephemeral data doesn't need to be backed up at all. It is regenerated as required, often without any intervention.

By contrast, business-critical data – the data upon which our business depends for survival – is of the highest priority to back up. A recommendation would be to have multiple, independent offsite backups of this data.

Business-operational data is the second-highest priority after the business-critical data.

Finally, normal data will be backed up if possible, but it has the lowest priority.

SUPER CONSULTING LTD

Let's look at our example company and see how its data is classified and what availability requirements it put on each element. The first step is to categorise every element of the data:

Business-critical data:

- Company internal wiki, which details the methodologies used

- Source code of the internally-developed BAT that the business uses

Business-operational data:

- Accounts system

- Contract management system

- Project management system

- HR system (employee manual, employment contracts, expenses forms, etc)

- Marketing data (brochures, company website, press releases, etc)

- Customer relationship management (CRM) system, including proposals

- Legal documents (NDAs, Terms and Conditions, contracts, etc)

- Operations manual

- Email system

- BAT system

Normal data:

- All contents of users' network home directories

- All contents of users' workstations

- The network 'scratch' share, used as temporary storage space

Note that the business-operational data list is much longer than the business-critical data list. This is to be expected: there is very little data that, if unavailable, would threaten the survival of the business.

The figure opposite considers these data categories from the perspective of recovery when unavailable. In the case of Super Consulting Ltd, the source code to its BAT represents its intellectual property, and thus a great deal of the value of the business is tied up in that code. If the source code were to become unavailable, it would be of critical importance to recover it. However, the business could weather an amount of time, probably measurable in days, without that source code being available, so long as it were ultimately restored. In other words, if the source code were unavailable, it would be important that it could be recovered, but the recovery time would not be urgent.

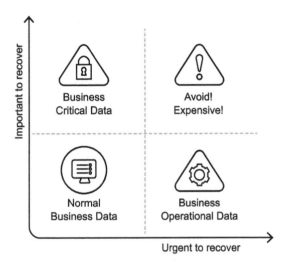

Important versus urgent data

By contrast, recovery of the project management system has a level of urgency about it. Projects are ongoing all the time, and the non-availability of the project management system will have an impact on today's work, so recovering the project management system would be considered urgent. If the project management system were not recoverable, it would have a serious impact on the business. It would lose credibility, maybe lose a client, and it would be embarrassing – but it's unlikely to end the life of the company.

The desired state, of course, is that all data is available all the time, and any outage can be corrected quickly and effectively. This analysis is not about what's ideal; rather, it is about putting priorities in place to help us deal with situations that are not ideal.

A word about the remaining two quadrants of the diagram in the figure above. Recovery of 'normal business data' is nice to have, but that is the extent of it. If Josh in Accounts loses his browser bookmarks, we should be able to recover them for him, but there is a modest limit on how much time and money we will invest in doing so.

Finally, the top-right area represents data that is both business-critical and urgent. For example, an airline flight booking system might fall into this category. A sustained failure in this area might put a smaller airline out of business, and even a relatively short-lived one could incur costs running into millions of pounds, as British Airways discovered in May 2017 when an IT failure led it to cancel most flights from Gatwick and Heathrow for a weekend (see *Resources*).[1] In short: either structure your business such that you avoid data in the top-right quadrant, or be prepared to invest heavily in preserving the availability of that data.

---

1   www.theguardian.com/business/2017/may/31/ba-it-shutdown-caused-by-uncontrolled-return-of-power-after-outage

Here's how our fictitious business, Super Consulting Ltd, defined its data availability requirements:

- Business-critical data must be recoverable within two working days. It must persist over multiple systems failures, including the failure of any one external entity, either physical (such as a data centre) or business (a supplier).

- Business-operational data must be recoverable within four business hours.

- Normal business data must be recoverable with two working days.

APPLICATIONS

The applications used to manage data can generally be considered to be available. Commercial applications can, worst case, be re-acquired; increasingly, applications are available online and their level of availability is out of your control. The exception is bespoke applications created specifically for your business, such as the BAT application above. Whether these are enhancements to existing applications to customise them, or they are built from scratch for you, the version you use is not readily available outside the context of your business. The source code to such applications should be treated as *data* rather than applications, and categorised accordingly.

SUMMARY

- Categorise your data and identify the critical data upon which your business depends
- Define appropriate recovery times for each category of data
- Custom code should be regarded as data

In this chapter, we've looked at categorising data by the impact of its loss. It's important to recognise that some data is more critical than other data: a blanket approach of backing up everything is suboptimal. The analysis of which data falls into which category is invaluable when we come to implement backups later in the book.

CHAPTER FOUR

Security Requirements

Like it or not, security is always a compromise. You want information to be available to the good guys as easily as possible, and not available to the bad guys at all. Every barrier that you put in place for the bad guys has the propensity to make life harder for the good guys too. Good security is about determining where to draw the line.

Our security requirements may be defined in a separate Security Policy document. A Security Policy is an integral part of ISO27001 (the Information Security Standard), so if you are ISO27001 certified, or are planning to be, you need a written Security Policy anyway. Like the other requirements, it serves as a checklist to ensure reality matches intent, and it provides clarity for those responsible for security. More than anything else, the process of writing the policy forces you to think through what is really needed.

This chapter covers the technical areas of a Security Policy. A full ISO27001 Security Policy needs to cover other areas as well, such as the vetting of suppliers, but the IT security policy is at the heart of an ISO27001 Security Policy document.

AUTHENTICATION

Authentication is how we know someone is who they claim to be. One common authentication technique is a username/password combination. It isn't 100% secure – we only know that someone (or something) has a valid username/password combination, not that they are who the username suggests they are – but it's a good starting point. Other authentication methods attempt to verify the identity of the user, and include biometric information (fingerprints, retina scans) and two-factor authentication (of which more in a moment).

There's a world of advice online about choosing a secure password, but in 2018 the most popular password was said to be '123456', closely followed by 'password'.[2] Your Security Policy should include the minimum requirement of a password. Here's what

---

2   https://en.wikipedia.org/wiki/List_of_the_most_common_
     passwords

Super Consulting Ltd defined, and, whilst it may not be right for you, it's a good starting point:

All user accounts must be password or passphrase protected. Passwords and passphrases must be a minimum of 8 characters and include at least four of the following:

- Upper case characters
- Lower case characters
- Numeric characters
- Punctuation characters
- Non-alphanumeric, non-punctuation characters (eg, '%', '@' or '*')

Passwords must not be written down. They may be retained electronically, provided that they are encrypted to at least 256-bit key Advanced Encryption Standard ('256-bit AES') and are protected by a password or passphrase that meets the above requirements.

Individual passwords and passphrases must not be divulged.

Some points to note:

- The use of non-alphanumeric characters. One traditional brute-force way to try to break into systems is the 'dictionary attack', where words from a dictionary are tried sequentially. Using non-alphanumeric characters makes such attacks more difficult.

43

- The use of password stores. These are ubiquitous, and represent a possible weakness in password security, so mandate under what circumstances they may be used.

- There's no requirement to change passwords periodically. Once a common recommendation, it is now recognised that this does little, if anything, to improve security. The National Cyber Security Centre, part of the Government Communications Headquarters, advises against mandating regular password changes.[3]

Increasingly common is two-factor authentication, or 2FA, which is considerably more secure than passwords alone and relatively easy to implement. The basis of 2FA is that the user *has* something (a physical device) and they *know* something. Both are required to authenticate. One example is online banking accounts that require their customers to use a mobile phone app and enter a passphrase to generate a single-use pass code.

The evolving Security Policy might be extended to say:

---

3   www.ncsc.gov.uk/guidance/password-guidance-simplifying-your-approach

Two-Factor Authentication is required for:

- Command line access to production servers
- Write access to the Company source code repository
- Edit access to the Company website

At the most basic level, each device – server, work-station, network switch, etc – uses its own authentication mechanism. This is how Linux systems are configured by default, but this is not in the least scalable. As soon as you have more than one system, you need to set up user accounts from scratch on each system. Any maintenance, such as adding or removing a user or resetting a password, also needs to be repeated on every system. A configuration management system, discussed in Chapter 9, can automate this task, but, no matter how it is managed, setting up independent accounts on each system is far from ideal.

Instead, a network-wide authentication is often used. Historically, systems such as 'Network Information Service' (NIS) or 'Yellow Pages' (YP) were used, but they have given way to the Lightweight Directory Access Protocol, or LDAP. This is supported by just about every Linux distribution as well as a great number of network devices and services. Many applications that require authentication can also be configured to use LDAP, meaning that the same credentials may be used to access all or most resources.

This unification of access credentials across devices and applications may be taken one stage further with Single Sign-On (SSO). With SSO, the act of authenticating once enables access to all authorised services without resupplying the access credentials. Microsoft Active Directory provides LDAP services, and thus it's possible to have a common authentication mechanism – including SSO if required – in a mixed environment of both Linux and Microsoft Windows. Very convenient for users, but considerably more complex to set up from both a system administration and application perspective.

Let's add that to Super Consulting's requirements, whilst recognising that not every resource may support network authentication:

Where possible, centralised authentication is to be used.

DATA AND NETWORK SECURITY

Looking after our data includes ensuring that it doesn't fall into the wrong hands. We can accomplish that primarily through some kind of access control or *authorisation* ('Only members of the board can access the five-year plan'), but there are situations where we may want to take more precautions:

- The data may be passing through an untrusted medium. That may be a network connection, particularly across the Internet; it may be a laptop that travels out and about and could be lost or stolen; it could be data stored on a USB key.

- The data may be so valuable or sensitive that we want to implement additional protection over and above our normal access control; for example, emails to HR will often contain sensitive information.

Under such circumstances, encryption can help. Encryption is the encoding of data so that it cannot be read by the casual observer. As children, we will have seen examples of encrypted messages, such as:

Gdkkn Vnqkc

That's 'Hello World', with each character substituted by the one preceding it in the alphabet. Of course, that's a trivial example; modern encryption techniques are complex and very secure. The most prevalent everyday use of encryption is in accessing websites via the 'https' protocol. With https, once the connection is established, all data passed between you and the remote web server is encrypted.

Traditionally, most everyday network services have not used encryption, and in many cases the communications between the user and the remote service use English-based text. Anyone with access to your network can look at the data being passed and could see (for example) a message from a server that says, 'Password:' and a few seconds later a reply, 'qwerty'. That applies to websites, email, file transfers and more. This is fundamentally insecure and has led to the rise in popularity of the 'secure', or encrypted, protocols, including:

- 'https', replacing 'http', for website traffic

- 'imaps', replacing 'imap', for reading email

- 'smtps', replacing 'smtp', for sending mail

- 'sftp', replacing 'ftp', for sending files

There's no reason not to mandate the use of secure network protocols for all access. If you host your own email server, an exception will be email (SMTP) connections between your server and others: if the remote email server doesn't offer an encrypted connection, you can't use an encrypted connection.

Let's add that to Super Consulting's policy:

Connections to company servers may only be via encrypted protocols. Exceptions:

- SMTP connections to and from external SMTP servers must use SMTPS where the third-party servers support such connections but may fall back to SMTP if necessary

- Connections within a server (ie, connections explicitly to the loopback address) via non-encrypted protocols are permitted

One final word on encryption. Encryption is often used in applications developed in-house. This is a good thing, but a word of warning: Do not write your own encryption routines. Writing secure encryption routines is incredibly hard. Even otherwise talented programmers have come unstuck working in this area, but, more to the point, there's no need. There exists a raft of routines and libraries that provide such services and can be incorporated into your applications. Those libraries are peer reviewed and kept up to date in a way that no individual or small team of programmers ever could.

Whereas we may be happy for any remote user to access our website, remote access to other resources may need more control. Typically this is achieved in part with a firewall, allowing, for example, open access to the web server but restricting who may access the file server. By far the most efficient way to control such access is via the remote network (IP) address. It is not 100% secure, but coupled with strong authentication it provides a good level of security.

Using the remote IP address to control access is challenging in part because many users will have a different address each time they try to connect. One approach is to open up the service to all and rely on authentication, but it is often far better to use a Virtual Private Network (VPN). Amongst other benefits, it's possible to mandate that remote access to a specific resource must be via a VPN.

COMPLIANCE

It is a requirement of ISO27001, and good practice anyway, to have some mechanism to ensure that the Security Policy is correctly implemented. Whilst the role of requirements is to specify *what* must be done rather than *how* it should be done, it is reasonable to say that monitoring should be in place. We might add the following to Super Consulting's policy:

SERVER MONITORING

All servers are to be monitored to ensure (as a minimum) that:

- All relevant security updates are installed in a timely fashion

- System backups are up to date and complete
- System performance is adequate for the role
- Security certificates have at least 10 days' validity
- The system clock is within 0.5 seconds of an Internet reference time source

The first of those, that relevant security updates are installed in a timely fashion, can be a challenging area, and one in which some organisations define exceptions to their policies to allow them to continue to run out-of-date software or older, unsupported, Linux distributions with known vulnerabilities. Typical reasons given for running such versions include, 'It still works fine for us', 'It would be too much effort to get all our applications working on the new version', and 'It's only used internally, so security doesn't matter'. That it still works fine is an attractive argument, similar to not going to the dentist for check-ups because your teeth 'still work fine'. Most would recognise the holes in that argument – not to mention in the teeth – which are perhaps best summed up for both Linux and teeth as: 'Prevention is better than cure'.

Given that older software has known, published, security vulnerabilities, the argument that it's 'too much effort' to upgrade a system begs the question, 'too much effort compared with what?'. If a system is compromised ('hacked'), the only sensible course of action is to rebuild it from the ground up.

Good system management includes being aware of what (possibly incompatible) changes are coming in later versions of the system software the business uses, and ensuring that business applications are compatible with those changes. Keeping up to date is a lot easier than playing catch up later, and it is a poor management strategy to elect to continue running out-of-date, unsupported, insecure software.

The last excuse, that the system is for internal use only and thus 'security doesn't matter', is worthy of deeper examination. There are three reasons why you should take internal security every bit as seriously as external security.

The first is pure malice: at some time, somewhere, there will be an employee who wants to try to do something they shouldn't. It doesn't matter why they want to do that: someone, someday, will try. The principle of only granting the minimum access and privileges required for each user to perform their role makes sense, and, coupled with keeping systems up to date, goes a long way to mitigating internal security threats from staff.

The second reason is viruses, malware and similar unpleasantries. Simply keeping your systems up to date does not guarantee that you won't be a victim of such things, but it will significantly help reduce the likelihood and impact of such events.

Lastly, there are third parties that have physical access to your network equipment, servers or workstations. They include cleaners, maintenance staff, those nearby if you have Wifi, visitors and possibly the building's owners. Keeping systems up to date and secure helps mitigate those threats.

In summary, stating within your requirements that all systems must be kept up to date with respect to security patches is highly recommended.

SUMMARY

- Define the requirements for passwords and passphrases

- Consider using two-factor authentication

- Mandate the use of secure network protocols

- Keep systems up to date

There are two written policies that every business should have with respect to security.

The first is the Security Policy, which has been discussed extensively above. The second is an Acceptable Use Policy (AUP), which sets out what users may and may not do with IT. There's an example of each on the *Resources* web page.

Security is a huge and complex subject, and we've only scratched the surface in this chapter. The aim of this chapter is to give a foundation and to raise awareness, but there will be other security considerations that apply to your business. The hard part is defining the security requirements in the first place. Updating them over time is considerably easier.

CHAPTER FIVE

Scalability

When a Linux infrastructure comprises multiple systems, it is important that the infrastructure is scalable. What do we mean by 'scalable'? The work required to set up the first few servers may be considerable, but within a scalable architecture, adding additional capacity – be that storage, compute power, desktop systems or users – should be far less expensive in terms of time and effort. For example, consider five servers that are available to a research department, all of which are configured identically. One day, Kate joins the research team. Someone now needs to log into each server in turn and set up a user account for her. As well as being time consuming, there may well be unintended differences between Kate's accounts on different servers. In this example, central user authentication can solve this problem. When Kate starts, a single user account is created for her, which enables her to log in at any system, and thus the administration of user authentication is scalable.

Scalability is more about how we think about systems than a checklist to follow. The key is that *adding capacity should be as frictionless as possible*. Here are some examples:

- Centralised user authorisation: one place from which all users can be managed. A new starter, a leaver, someone who now needs access to the 'marketing' file share – go to one place to manage them all.

- Centralised system management: a configuration management system (discussed further in Chapter 9), that allows changes made in one place to be propagated across all (or a defined subset of) systems. It helps ensure consistency between systems and makes it trivial to build a server that is similar to an existing one.

- Centralised network management: manage network addresses from one location, whether automatically (by using services such as Dynamic Host Configuration Protocol – DHCP), or perhaps an IP Address Management (IPAM) tool, such as NIPAP.

- Resource sharing: if all workstations are built identically, any user can use any workstation. For businesses that run a series of long-lasting automated jobs, rather than have users manually locate a free system to run jobs on, use a grid engine such as Open Grid Scheduler.

- Consistency: use the same Linux distribution on all systems. That may not always be possible, but at least have a default, and ensure that other distributions are only used when justified.

- Good systems architecture: servers can only be expanded so far in terms of CPU power, memory and disk. Scalability means you can continue to increase the amount of compute power, storage, etc, that's available without having to throw away the existing servers and replace them with bigger ones.

For businesses with multiple sites, 'centralised' may mean 'centralised per location', but the principle remains the same.

One area that is sometimes overlooked with respect to scalability is data storage. A small number of large dedicated data stores on a network is generally preferable to each server managing its own data storage. Often one data store per location will be enough. Consolidating data in this way gives a number of benefits:

- Spare capacity: when data is stored in multiple locations, the free space is also spread over multiple locations. This can lead to unnecessary (and error-prone) moving of data from one location to another in order to have sufficient free space for a new project.

- Benefits of scale: having multiple disks in one location can give better performance and resilience than multiple smaller data stores in separate locations. Adding more disks to a single store means that the data storage for all users is increased.

- Clarity: if there is one data store, there is only one place to go for data.

- Focus: the data storage system can be designed and optimised purely for data storage rather than having to compromise by also running other business applications.

- Backups: there is only one data store, which greatly simplifies backups.

The exception to this rule is databases. Although they do, of course, store data, that data is intimately related to, and used by, just one application: the database software itself. It is appropriate to configure database software and the associated storage as one entity.

As soon as you have more than a couple of servers, a centralised data store is a much more efficient way to store data, as the following example illustrates. Having decided on one data store, that is where the definitive version of our data should be stored, rather than on desktop, laptop or mobile devices. The latter are built for convenience and to a budget. They are great for manipulating the data, but the technology they use to store data will seldom be resilient.

A bioscience company had five compute servers. These were highly-specified systems: lots of CPU power, lots of memory and lots of disk space. Over time, the disk space was slowly consumed. Some older projects had archive data remaining, and newer projects generated a lot more data than older projects. The situation came to a head when it was realised that, although there was sufficient free disk space between the five servers for a new project, no one server had sufficient space. A complex and time-consuming exercise was undertaken, moving data between various systems to make sufficient space available on one server for the new project. Even then, the problem is not solved for subsequent projects. If the decision is made to provide additional storage for each server, the unused space will still be distributed between the servers, ultimately leading to a repeat of data being moved around to make space. These servers, and specifically the data storage areas, were not scalable.

The solution was to set up a storage cluster. The only role of this cluster was to provide data storage for the other systems. Now all the storage is consolidated in one place. When available space runs low, the storage cluster can be upgraded, and the problem is solved. The storage cluster itself stores the data on a fault-tolerant, high-performance disk array, and the whole system is configured as a high-availability cluster to provide resilience against server failure.

HARDWARE

Good performance of a Linux system depends upon the availability of four key resources:

- CPU

- Memory

- Storage bandwidth

- Network bandwidth

These are largely independent of each other. In other words, if the disks are working flat out then it doesn't matter how much memory you have available – the system performance will suffer. Having said that, there are some interdependencies. When free memory is getting low, one technique contemporary operating systems use is *swapping*, sometimes called *paging*. Swapping involves copying areas of memory to disk, thus freeing the memory for other programs. The process can be reversed when the swapped-out data is required for use. Disk access is orders of magnitude slower than memory access, so whilst a nominal amount of swapping is normal and healthy, excessive swapping is not a long-term solution to an under-resourced system.

Conversely, poor disk performance may be somewhat alleviated by memory. By allocating areas of memory to be used as disk buffers, the number of read and write operations to disk may be reduced, which can yield a small performance increase.

The specification for CPU and memory depends very much upon the role of the server, but in terms of requirements it is prudent to allow some spare capacity. It is significantly cheaper, in terms of both finances and disruption costs, to over-specify memory and CPU capacity when a system is commissioned than to increase them retrospectively. This is less applicable in the case of cloud computing where resources are rented by the hour or minute.

Here's what Super Consulting Ltd added to its Requirements in relation to these capabilities:

- The main page of the Business Analysis Tool must render within 2 seconds
- A search for a company name with the BAT must return the full list of matching companies within 2 seconds

SUMMARY

- Consider how systems may grow in the future
- Where possible, centralise data storage amongst your servers

In this section, we've looked at techniques that may be used to ensure that your Linux infrastructure remains scalable. Some of the ideas presented straddle the line between requirements and implementation, but the thinking process when specifying requirements is key to building a scalable infrastructure. With practice, it's possible to recognise ideas that are not scalable.

CHAPTER SIX

Other Requirements

The requirements we've considered so far may be viewed as being idealistic. The idea of a fully redundant, high-performance, high-capacity file storage cluster may be attractive, but is it affordable? In the real world, we may be limited by other factors.

CONSTRAINTS

Constraints are external conditions that limit our choices, and by 'external' I mean external to the IT infrastructure planning process. For example, it might be corporate policy to buy all server hardware from a specific vendor. Such a constraint is not a true requirement; it is an implementation detail. Rather than state that it is a requirement that hardware must be supplied by Acme Ltd, list it as a constraint.

GIVENS

Some requirements may be reasonably assumed. For example, all other factors being equal, a cheaper option will be preferred over a more expensive option. In reality, though, 'all other factors' are seldom equal. Even choosing a commodity supplier on the basis of price may have implications around delivery times, warranty and any returns process.

REPORTING

Some requirements may be non-negotiable due to legal or regulatory obligations. Many of these obligations conform with best practice anyway, but it's worth highlighting the reason for them in your Requirements Document. There will almost certainly be a requirement that you are able to demonstrate compliance, which in turn may impose reporting requirements. If you are a service organisation, you may have an SLA with your customers. The ability to measure performance against an SLA will in turn impose reporting requirements. The demand for reports varies hugely between different organisational cultures, so it's helpful to define and agree from the outset what reports are required.

Other than those produced for legal or conformance reasons, the key question to answer for any report that will be generated is, 'How will it be used?' (or, more bluntly, 'What will you do with it?'). It's easy to produce reports that show how much free disk space there is on a server or how many emails were received or identified as having viruses, but is that information likely to precipitate action that would otherwise not have occurred? Being aware that available disk space is becoming critical may be important, but a weekly report is not an appropriate way to communicate the problem.

If the report is 'for information only', it's questionable whether it has any value at all. If the report will be scanned for any departures from the norm, then, rather than have a report, define the parameters that are acceptable – for example, disks must not be more than 80% full – and use a monitoring system to do the job. Such a system will check all disks (and myriad other parameters) and will generate an alert if those parameters fall outside defined limits. The alert will be seen by someone in a position to rectify the problem. We'll talk a lot more about monitoring later.

The aim of some reports is to show what work is being done by the IT staff. There may be some value here, but trend information is more valuable than absolute numbers. For example, knowing that there were 211 new support tickets last week is largely meaningless, whereas a graph showing the number of new tickets per week over the last year may be more useful. More useful still might be a graph of how many open tickets there are at the end of each day over the course of a year.

Reports that demonstrate compliance with either a standard (eg, ISO27001) or a regulatory framework are, of course, specific to the standard. We won't go into details here other than to say that if you need to provide such reports, ensure that they are listed in your Requirements Document.

There's another type of report which is often very simple in format, and which just reports the status of a regular job. For example, it may be an email that says, 'Backups ran successfully'. This immediately fails the 'What are you going to do with it?' test ('delete it' means it wasn't worth receiving in the first place). If the mail fails to arrive one morning, will you notice? Again, this is a monitoring function that is best delegated to a monitoring system.

It can be useful to make status information available throughout the business or, in some cases, to customers and even the general public. Many ISPs and SAAS (Software As A Service) companies will have a 'status page' on their website that lists any significant issues they are aware of. This is helpful for their users, and it will also reduce the number of calls to the helpdesk if users can see that you're already aware of (and are taking steps to resolve) the issue.

It's easy to get carried away with reports. The aim of reports is to improve the business in some way, and reports that are not read or do not result in action fail to meet that aim. From a reports perspective, fewer is often better.

Whilst I'm a strong advocate of defining requirements before starting implementation, it's usually straightforward to add reports later. It's also often the case that the *real* information required in a report only becomes apparent after some time: over-engineering the perfect report on day one may turn out to be a waste of time.

For each report requested or generated, consider the following and update the Requirements Document as appropriate:

- What action will the recipient take as a result of receiving the report?

- Could the report data be better interpreted by an automated monitoring system?

- Should this information be made more widely available, perhaps via a status page?

SUMMARY

- List external constraints as such rather than as requirements

- Ensure that the function of reports is not better handled by appropriate monitoring

- Reports should only be produced to either meet regulatory requirements or to precipitate specific actions

Writing a Requirements Document is an undertaking that is much harder than it initially appears. What at first seems straightforward develops more layers as more detail is considered.

Don't try to write it alone. You're unlikely to consider every aspect of your IT infrastructure, and a second pair of eyes will often identify missing components. There are also different viewpoints: the infrastructure must serve the business, be used by users and supported in some way, and each of those considerations will influence the requirements.

Whilst in development, it should be emphasised that anything within the Requirements Document may be changed. However, once the requirements have been agreed, recognise that any subsequent changes have a cost. Not only may there be a financial cost in having to discard work done that is no longer required, but there's also an emotional cost.

No one wants to think their work and effort have been wasted, and equally no one wants to revisit the same points around requirements repeatedly. Once you've made the decision, document it and move on.

Remember, the focus of the Requirements Document is just that: requirements. It should not contain implementation details – focus on *what*, not *how*. It's inevitable that you'll consider some implementation details as you write the Requirements Document, and they can be noted for later, but do not make implementation part of the Requirements Document. This is a very easy and very common mistake to make. Similarly, the word 'should' has no place in a Requirements Document; this is requirements, not suggestions.

Writing the Requirements Document can feel tedious. Sometimes it is hard, and the temptation can be to skip this step: after all, you know you need a file server, so why not just get on with putting one in place? The reality, of course, is that at some point and in some way the requirements *will* be established. It will be far better in the long run to take some time to think them through, document them and get consensus before you start implementation. Then you have a document that not only represents an internally agreed uniform vision of what you are trying to achieve but also one that can be shown to suppliers so that they understand the big picture, too.

SECTION TWO
IMPLEMENTATION

Now that we've defined our requirements, we can turn to implementation. The aim of implementation is to design and build systems that are capable of meeting the requirements. The options open to us have changed dramatically over the past decade. In this section, we'll look at a variety of possibilities from the traditional standalone hardware, through cloud computing services up to contemporary container orchestration solutions. Each approach has its pros and cons, and we'll examine them all.

Of all the elements in the RISE methodology, it's the Implementation phase that is the most technical. Designing and building effective IT infrastructures requires in-depth knowledge of the technologies available, and they change rapidly, particularly in the cloud space. If you need more help, consider the use of an independent systems architect. Vendors can also be helpful, but they understandably will have a limit to the range of solutions they may present.

CHAPTER SEVEN

Linux Distributions

Before we look at how we'll run Linux, we need to look at which Linux distribution we will run. There are, literally, hundreds of Linux distributions out there, so how do you choose the most appropriate one for your business? For some, constraints such as corporate policy or the application software vendor may reduce or even eliminate choice, but for many the decision is more open.

Although the versions of the software used will vary, the vast majority of Linux distributions centre around the Linux kernel, which is the heart of the system. Much of the supporting software (operating system utilities, application programs, etc) are also common amongst most Linux distributions; for example, the popular web server Apache is available on just about every Linux distribution. Each distribution has features that differentiate it from the others, but most of the differences come down to one or more of the following five aspects:

1. AVAILABILITY OF VENDOR SUPPORT

A few distributions are created, maintained and supported by commercial companies; for example, Red Hat and SUSE Linux. If, for whatever reason, vendor support is important to you, your choice of distributions is very limited. Bear in mind that lack of vendor support does not mean there is no support available: there are plenty of third-party support options for those distributions. If you do choose to use vendor support, remember too that they will support *only* their distribution. If you end up using multiple distributions, you may need multiple support channels.

The Linux distributions that offer vendor support are, almost by definition, large companies themselves. That has both positive and negative aspects, but, unless you too represent a large company, you may find that they lack the in-depth knowledge of your infrastructure. On the positive side, some skilled Linux engineers are naturally attracted to such organisations, and it would be reasonable to expect that they have deep understanding of how to use that particular distribution in a business setting.

Some software application vendors will only support their products on specific Linux distributions. This does not mean that their products will not work on other distributions – far from it – but if support from the software vendor itself is important to you, this again will restrict your choice of distribution.

There are many companies other than the vendors who will provide support services, and there's certainly no reason to believe that the vendor will always provide the most appropriate support package for every business. For some, vendor support for either an application or the Linux distribution itself is a non-negotiable requirement, but for everyone else there are probably more important considerations when it comes to choosing external help. We'll look at this in more detail in Chapter 22.

2. RANGE OF SOFTWARE AVAILABLE

Software for Linux is typically provided in 'packages', and the number of packages available varies greatly between distributions. For example, at the time of writing Red Hat Enterprise Linux has nearly 20,000 packages available whereas Debian has almost three times that number – but if Red Hat Enterprise Linux has all the software you need, it could still be the right choice.

The package count may be deceptive. Using the same distributions as an example, Debian favours multiple smaller packages to enable more granular installations whereas Red Hat tends more towards larger 'kitchen sink included' packages. Neither is better; they're just different philosophies.

The major distributions generally include all of the packages typically needed by a business, but if you are aware that you have specific, less common requirements, this is an area to check. The starting point should be a list of software requirements, against which various distributions may be assessed.

It is possible to install software not packaged by the distributor, but there are a number of potential pitfalls to be aware of if you choose this route:

- The application may have dependencies on other software which may also not be packaged for your chosen distribution. What starts off as a requirement to install one additional application can quickly snowball into many such applications.

- Worse, the application may have dependencies on other software that *is* packaged by your chosen distribution, but where the vendor-packaged version is incompatible with the new application. Upgrading the installed supporting software may break other software that depends specifically on the original version.

- Software obtained from somewhere other than the Linux vendor may be of less trustworthy provenance.

- Software that isn't provided by the Linux distribution will not, of course, be included in the distribution security updates, so you'll need to ensure that you have a mechanism in place to keep such software updated.

- There may be interoperability issues between the 'foreign' software and the Linux distribution software. Other than version requirements, discussed above, this is unlikely. However, if a system is misbehaving in unusual or subtle ways, it may become necessary to remove the non-distribution software to see whether that is having an adverse impact.

All of the above pitfalls can be overcome, but they increase the complexity of the system, which in turn tends to increase the cost of ownership.

3. FOCUS

Some distributions focus on the desktop (eg, Fedora, Mint), some on the server (Debian, Red Hat), and still others on a specific sector (Scientific Linux, 64 Studio). Distributions that focus on the server market tend to make stability a priority, and thus they will usually prefer slightly older, more proven, versions of software over the newer versions with shorter track records. By contrast, distributions aimed at the desktop may have newer versions of some software, and they will typically include as standard utilities aimed at users, such as those for playing music or editing videos.

Some distributions are happy to include software that does not fall under the Open Source banner, whereas others are more conservative. Such closed-source software includes utilities such as CODECs, used for decoding various proprietary video and audio formats, and certain network and video drivers. In many cases, that software can still be installed, but the user has to specifically acknowledge that they want to use 'non-free' software.

4. SYSTEM MANAGEMENT UTILITIES

The ways in which the software packages are put together vary, although many distributions use either the Red Hat or the Debian format. The package management tools will necessarily be different, depending on the format used, and some distributions include additional system management tools of their own. However, this is usually only of interest to the system administrator: the underlying application and system software will be the same. This can be an emotive area for system administrators:

for every SysAdmin that prefers Red Hat, there will be another who will insist that the Debian system is better.

5. SECURITY UPDATE POLICY

As with all software, Linux systems have security patches released from time to time. The major distributions are generally very good at getting patches out in good time, but this can be one area where the less mainstream distributions fail.

This is an important area, and it's discussed more in Chapter 19. For now, if you choose to use a distribution other than those listed later in this chapter, your process of due diligence should include checking the timeliness of recent security updates from your chosen distributions.

SHOULD YOU EVEN CARE?

You may not care about the specific Linux distribution used, but you should be consistent. It may be appropriate to be using more than one distribution within the organisation, but each additional one imposes cost in terms of support, compatibility and user training. If you use multiple distributions, at least ensure that that is a conscious choice, unlike in the example below.

An engineering company employed around
20 software engineers, each using a Linux
workstation. The company policy was that each
engineer could run whatever Linux distribution they
wanted with the aim of keeping everyone happy.

The result was chaotic. Each engineer could
work effectively on only their own workstation
as the others were unknown environments.
Worse, because of different system software
versions, a program compiled on one workstation
often wouldn't even run on another. Organising
independent software testing was a nightmare.

After a period of analysis, the company
implemented Debian Linux on every workstation
and the problems disappeared overnight. Some
engineers were initially upset at the change,
but care was taken to ensure their individual
requirements were met wherever possible.
The resulting increase in productivity easily
compensated for the short-term pain.

If nothing else, it is helpful to understand the differences between the various distributions, which allows a more meaningful discussion to be had with those who are supporting or managing your systems.

WHAT'S BEST FOR BUSINESS?

A distribution that is appropriate for business use needs to have:

- An excellent record of getting security updates out in a timely fashion

- Support services available, either from the vendor or credible third parties

- Suitable business software packaged as part of the distribution

- A pedigree: you probably don't want to bet your business on a distribution that was first released last year

- A reasonable user base size

Despite the hundreds of distributions available, only a handful are serious contenders for the general business case. Given the nature of Open Source software, it is impossible to definitively state which distributions are the most popular in businesses, but experience suggests that the following comprise 90% or more of commercial Linux installations (links to each are on the *Resources* page):

- Red Hat Enterprise Linux ('RHEL')

- CentOS ('Community ENTerprise Operating System')

- Debian

- Ubuntu

Let's consider each in turn.

Red Hat Enterprise Linux

Red Hat Inc is a US company that provides Red Hat Enterprise Linux, together with support, consultancy and training services based around Red Hat solutions. Red Hat formed in 1993, and at the time it was one of a handful of organisations making Linux distributions available to the public (in their case, 'Red Hat Linux'). The company changed gear with the first release of RHEL – version 2.1, in 2002 – which was aimed squarely at the enterprise market. The original Red Hat Linux releases stopped in 2003 when it was merged into Fedora Linux. In 2018, Red Hat was acquired by IBM. At the time of writing, soon after that acquisition, it isn't clear what, if any, impact the acquisition will have.

The majority of commercial Linux software that specifies a Linux distribution will be certified for RHEL, although that software can almost always be run on other Linux distributions.

Red Hat Enterprise Linux – like all Linux distributions – is Open Source software, which means the source must be made freely available. Part of Red Hat's revenue is derived from selling copies of

RHEL, but therein lies a problem. If the software is Open Source, it would be legitimate for a business to buy one copy and copy it to use everywhere. To protect its revenue, Red Hat incorporates its logos into the RHEL distribution. Red Hat owns the copyright for their logos, which are also registered trademarks, and thus Red Hat Inc is able to define the conditions under which the logos may be used, including making copies, thus protecting their revenue stream. This brings us nicely to CentOS.

CentOS

CentOS, the 'Community ENTerprise Operating System', is essentially RHEL minus the Red Hat branding and logos. The CentOS engineers take the Open Source Red Hat code, strip out the parts that may not be redistributed, and package the remainder with their own branding. Although the history goes back a little further, the first release of CentOS, version 3, was made in 2004.

Unlike RHEL, CentOS is freely available to be downloaded, copied, distributed, etc. In 2014, perhaps surprisingly, CentOS announced that it was joining forces with Red Hat, with some of the core members of the CentOS team being employed by Red Hat. Ironically, Red Hat now owns the CentOS logos. The CentOS project is a community project managed by the CentOS Governing Board, and CentOS itself relies on donations from users and sponsors.

Debian

Debian is an independent Linux distribution managed by the *Debian Project*, which is a voluntary group. For some, the notion of trusting their IT infrastructure, let alone their intellectual property, to a distribution run by volunteers is anathema. But – and it's a big but – it works. Debian is one of the oldest Linux distributions, first released in 1993, and it has spawned many child distributions, not least of all Ubuntu, one of the best-known Linux distributions.

If one considers professionalism to be a behaviour rather than an indication of payment, Debian is a rock-solid, reliable, professionally-managed Linux distribution with almost 60,000 software packages freely available. There are many large corporations in which Debian plays a significant role. There is no 'Debian Inc' or 'Debian plc', and thus no vendor support available, but there are plenty of third-party companies that support Debian.

Ubuntu

Ubuntu is a Debian-based distribution that was first released in late 2004. At that time it was aimed at the desktop market, and it has arguably done more to bring Linux to the attention of the general public than any other distribution. New releases are made every six months, each based on the next upcoming Debian version. As such, it tends to have newer software packages available than some other distributions, although care should be taken not to confuse 'newer' with 'better'.

Ubuntu is backed by a commercial company, the UK-based Canonical Ltd. The Ubuntu distribution is freely available, with Canonical providing optional paid support and consultancy services. Canonical also has other revenue streams, although at the time of writing the company is not yet profitable.

Build your own Linux distribution

A few years ago, there was a trend amongst companies to build their own Linux distributions for internal use. If you take only one thing from this book, let it be this: *don't do it*. Maintaining your own distribution is opening the door to a world of pain. Any of the four distributions above will be multiple orders of magnitude better at distribution maintenance, and that applies whether you're a one-man band just starting up or an international corporation.

If you're still not convinced, please go and find three experienced, serious Linux consultants, buy some of their time, explain what you want to do and why, and ask them what they think.

SO HOW DO YOU CHOOSE?

Consistency is a good place to start. If you feel that you should use Red Hat for the production environment, then use Red Hat everywhere. It's not uncommon to see businesses use Red Hat for production but CentOS for development or UAT in an attempt to save money. Red Hat and CentOS are very similar, but they are not identical, and this may cause problems at some point.

An exception to the consistency rule may be the distinction between desktop and server. Non-technical users may find a desktop-oriented system more friendly than a server-oriented one – but make sure your developers are using the same system as your servers. In reality, it's probably easier to use the same distribution everywhere and tweak the setup for desktop users.

If there is someone in your organisation who is responsible for supporting the Linux infrastructure, then they should be involved in the distribution selection process. Ask them for recommendations as to which distribution would be most appropriate, and – importantly – ask them why they are making that recommendation. If you don't have anyone in place at the moment, you may want to read Chapter 22 before proceeding.

Still not sure? Use Debian.

SUMMARY

• Stick to one Linux distribution where possible

• Ensure your chosen distribution has a record of releasing security updates in good time

• Don't build your own distribution

Ultimately, Linux is Linux. In the same way as a Ford and a BMW provide fundamentally the same services, so it is with Linux distributions. There's a lot to be said for using a mainstream distribution as listed above, but get the buy-in of the support staff first.

CHAPTER EIGHT

Data Storage

For most businesses, data is the reason for having IT systems in the first place. Data might include the contents of a website, a database, a research paper, an engineering specification, programming code, client lists and more. In this chapter, we're going to look at the considerations for storing and managing that data.

There are two key considerations when it comes to storing data: *where* it is stored, and *how* it is stored. As discussed in Chapter 5, ideally all data is stored in one location, and that should be in a server room, in a data centre or with a cloud provider. Such an environment will benefit from:

- Stable power that is backed by an uninterruptible power supply (UPS)

- Being air conditioned to an appropriate temperature and humidity

- Network connections that are fast with multiple routes

- More space available to hold additional storage, possibly configured in such a way as to improve resilience, speed or both

- Having physical access to the servers tightly controlled and monitored

That's where we want to keep our data: where it has the best chance of surviving. For our day-to-day work, we either access that data on the server over the network or we create a local copy to work with.

DISK PERFORMANCE

Our data is almost invariably stored on disks, although those disks might be 'Solid State Disks' (SSDs). SSDs aren't really disks at all; rather, they are solid-state devices that use persistent memory to store data. 'Solid-state' means no moving parts; 'persistent' means that the memory used retains the data stored when the power is removed – unlike the main system memory in a computer system – and 'disk' is simply a description of the interface used to connect the SSD to the rest of the system. From the system's perspective, the SSD looks exactly like a disk. SSDs are reliable and fast, but they are still significantly more expensive than traditional rotating media and still lack the capacity of the larger traditional disks. A well-designed Redundant Array of Independent Disks (RAID) subsystem (see the next subsection below) using rotating media will beat the performance of non-RAID SSDs.

The rate at which data can be read from and written to storage is often the limiting factor in a system's performance. When using traditional (rotating media) disks, two key factors influence that rate:

- Rotational speed: Before data can be written to or read from a disk, the correct part of the disk has to appear under the disk read/write heads. The time spent waiting for the disk to turn is called 'rotational latency'. The faster disks rotate, the lower the rotational latency and the faster data can be read from or written to the disk.

- On-disk cache: As well as disk buffers in the operating system and caching on the disk controller, rotating disks also have a built-in cache. Holding the data to be written in local memory allows the disk to optimise the order in which various bits of data are written, which helps to reduce rotational latency. The larger the on-disk cache, the better the ultimate performance.

There are techniques that aim to take the higher-speed SSDs and use them as a caching layer in front of the slower (and cheaper) rotating disks in an attempt to get the best of both worlds. This can show some performance improvements with smaller numbers of rotating disks, but as the number of rotating disks grows, the performance they alone can offer approaches that of the hybrid solutions.

Such hybrid solutions are always a compromise, and they rarely stand the test of time. They also introduce more complexity, and commercial IT infrastructures are not crying out for additional complexity. It's likely that SSDs will become cheaper per unit storage over time, their capacity will grow and they may well become the storage media of choice. For now, a well-designed RAID array using rotating media and a high-end hardware RAID card will give excellent performance.

Both rotating media and SSDs are available in 'consumer-grade' and 'enterprise-grade' versions. The latter are designed to be active 24/7 and to have a longer (and harder) working life. As might be expected, they have a corresponding price tag. In general, enterprise-grade disk storage is worth the additional cost.

RAID SYSTEMS

Research by Google suggests that, for disks aged one to five years, an annual failure rate between 5% and 9% is realistic (see *Resources*).[4] If your data store comprises fourteen drives – a very modest number of disks – you should expect around one failure per year.

RAID is a technique for combining multiple disks into one logical storage unit. There are various RAID techniques, but each aims to provide one or more of the following advantages over a single disk:

- Reliability: Some RAID systems can tolerate the failure of one or more physical disk drives without loss of data or significant impact upon performance

- Performance: With multiple disks, rotational latency can be reduced

- Capacity: Individual drives can be amalgamated to present a logically larger capacity

Wikipedia has a summary of the different types of RAID plus more detailed descriptions of each (see *Resources*).[5] RAID techniques may either be implemented as part of the operating system or delegated

---

4   https://static.googleusercontent.com/media/research.google.com/en//archive/disk_failures.pdf
5   https://en.wikipedia.org/wiki/RAID

to a dedicated disk controller. Dedicated controllers bring a number of advantages:

- On-board caching: Data just read or waiting to be written may be stored in memory on the RAID controller itself rather than using up valuable system memory.

- Battery-backed cache: Data intended to be written to disk will be stored for a very short time in memory on the controller. In the event of a system power failure, that data would normally be lost, and thus the safe way of configuring such a system is for the RAID controller to only confirm to the operating system that the operation is complete once the writing has actually taken place. By providing a battery-backed cache, which uses a small battery on the RAID controller to power the cache memory, it is safe to configure the controller to say the data has been written to disk as soon as it is in the controller cache ('write through caching'). This results in a significant increase in data throughput.

- Offloading work: Calculating what data should be placed on which drives (which is complex for some RAID configurations) can be carried out by the RAID controller without imposing additional load on the operating system.

In short, for any system where significant reading and writing to disk is expected, a well-configured hardware RAID controller is often a cost-effective way of getting a significant performance improvement.

DISK FAILURES

As mentioned above, most RAID systems can mitigate against individual disk failures. However, when a failed disk is replaced, the new disk needs to be populated with data in order to maintain the resilience of the overall data store, and that in turn imposes an atypically high load on the remaining disks. There is a tendency when building RAID arrays to take multiple disks produced by the same vendor at the same time, but this isn't necessarily the best strategy as it can give rise to two possible problems:

- It's likely that all disks would come from the same batch and thus have a similar lifespan, increasing the likelihood of simultaneous disk failure, particularly during the higher-stress workload following a disk replacement.

- If there is a problem in that batch that increases the chance of failure, this increased risk would apply to all disks in the array and therefore to the array itself.

Certain RAID configurations can be tolerant of multiple simultaneous disk failures. Although there is a higher cost to implementing such configurations, the cost is contained in one place (the single data store) rather than on every server. It's also possible to configure 'hot spares', disks that are not used for data storage until a disk failure is detected. At that time, the failed disk is taken offline and the data rebuild is started on one of the hot spares (which now, of course, is no longer a spare). All of this can take place automatically, and thus the time when the data store has reduced redundancy is minimised.

Although redundant disks can be fitted as described above, they won't help if the underlying hardware experiences a catastrophic failure. That would be a very unusual occurrence, particularly with fault-tolerant hardware, but it's not unheard of. To mitigate against this, it's possible to replicate an entire data store. Two data stores are built and configured such that at any one time one is 'live' and the other 'standby'. As data is updated on the live side, it is replicated in near-real-time to the standby data store. If the live data store goes offline, this is detected and the standby store – fully up to date – is brought online to replace it. Again, this process is fully automated. The example below shows how a business might implement such replication.

Like many technology businesses, this one was utterly reliant upon its data. The value of the business was contained within that data as code representing the intellectual property. All of its Linux infrastructure, including all data, was held on site in a secure server room.

Any lack of availability of the data would have a serious impact upon project schedules, so the decision was made to fully replicate the data store. Rather than just implementing a simple replication, the decision was taken to put each half of the data store in a separate server room with a dedicated fibre link between them for replication. That way, even if one server room fails in some way – perhaps multiple air conditioner failures – the business can continue to access all of its data.

MANAGING STORAGE

Once built, the RAID array can present a large amount of storage with good performance and built-in resilience against disk failure. How do we use that large data storage effectively? Over time the data storage requirements for the various parts of the system will change, typically growing in size, but the different areas of data storage may grow at different rates.

The Linux Logical Volume Manager (LVM) can take the underlying disk storage system presented to the operating systems and – as the name suggests – create logical volumes of data. The trick here is not to allocate all the space available on day one. If you expect all data areas to grow at approximately the same rate, you may want to initially allow 50% free space. Today you might have 2.5TB of test data, so you allocate 4TB to that area, and so on. That may leave you with 11TB of unallocated space, but one of the advantages of LVM is that it is trivially easy to grow a logical volume. When your test data needs to unexpectedly double in size, you can add another 3TB to it.

It is significantly harder to shrink a logical volume, so if the data on one volume grows much less than expected, significant work is needed to reclaim that space for use elsewhere. Being initially conservative with the storage allocation is a good policy.

As a general guideline, you should aim to keep those logical volumes at no more than 80% capacity. Linux is extraordinarily good at managing the way disk space is allocated to files, but as the volume becomes fuller it is harder to avoid file fragmentation, which leads to lower performance.

SUMMARY

- A well-configured disk subsystem with a dedicated hardware RAID controller will give excellent performance

- SSDs should be used for small, high-speed data stores

- Allocate raw storage space to Logical Volumes on an 'as required' basis

In this chapter, we've looked at how data may be stored and managed. We've looked at the media the data is stored on, and we spent some time looking at techniques that can both speed up data access and offer some resilience over disk hardware failure. Finally, we looked at how to manage that large data store into smaller chunks for actually storing our data.

Configuration Management

Maintaining a Linux infrastructure includes making changes to systems over time – removing a user, adding a new application, updating a certificate, and so on. Logging in to each server in turn and updating it is one way to make these changes; using some kind of automation is another way. In this chapter, we are going to discuss automating such processes using a configuration management system (CMS). For clarity, in this context the abbreviation 'CMS' refers only to a configuration management system as opposed to any other meaning.

In discussions of CMSs, you may come across the following terms:

- Configuration management system (CMS): the term we will use

- Configuration management software: the software that implements a CMS

- Software configuration management: this term is more accurately applied to the tracking of changes to specific software rather than the system as a whole

- Orchestration: the creation and management of computer systems, often including billing, and typically used in a cloud computing context

We won't look at the subtle differences between each of those terms, only at the central control of system configuration as a whole.

The principle of a CMS is straightforward. There are one or more central 'CMS servers', and there are the systems that they manage – the 'CMS clients'. Periodically, the configuration of the client is checked against a template held on the server. If the actual configuration of the client differs from that defined in the template, the necessary changes are made to the client such that it conforms to the template.

Almost any aspect of the client configuration may be controlled by a CMS server; for example:

- The installation or removal of a software package

- The creation or removal of a user account

- The addition and configuration of a new website

- A change to the firewall rules

- System tuning settings

- Setting passwords

A CMS may seem like overkill if you only have two servers, and whilst it is true that the value increases with the number of systems, there is some sense in starting early when the implementation will be simpler. Benefits in consistency, accountability and cost management can be realised almost immediately:

- Consistency: If we define a change that must be made to all web servers, a CMS will ensure that the same change is made on each. Any little extras that are needed – a tweak to a configuration file, the reloading of an application – will also happen on all servers.

- Accountability: An audit trail of changes (who, what, when) can easily be created if the configuration data on the CMS server is stored in a version control system.

- Cost Management: With a CMS, changes to multiple target systems only have to be implemented once. The value of that cost saving will, of course, depend on how many servers are affected, but without a CMS the likelihood of errors being made, with consequential costs, increases with the number of servers.

The servers across the estate will have different configurations, and there are multiple ways to select which clients any specific configuration parameters should be applied to. CMS clients have a degree of introspection, so it's possible to say, 'Enable this software repository for all systems running Red Hat Enterprise Linux version 7'. It's straightforward to add user-defined selection parameters, so we can say 'Add user "james" to all systems that have a role of "development"'.

Abstraction is also possible. For example, to install the Apache web server on a Red Hat system, the package name to install is 'httpd', whereas on a Debian system it's 'apache2'. We can tell the CMS that all servers in group 'web servers' should have Apache installed, and the CMS can take care of the exact package name needed as well as the appropriate commands required to install it on a given system.

The hassle of manually logging into fifteen web servers to install a new Apache module and trusting that each and every installation will be the same has gone. The process now is simply to update the list of packages that should be installed on every web server, and leave the rest to the CMS.

All of the files that control client configuration should be kept in a revision control system, providing an audit trail of changes made. Here's a simplified version of the workflow we use at Tiger Computing:

- A request for change is logged on the ticketing system.

- The required changes are staged and tested using a test environment.

- Once finalised, a request is generated with details of the proposed change, justification, completed testing and documentation.

- The proposed change is independently checked and, if approved, merged to the production environment. The 'commit' message includes the original ticket number.

- The ticket is automatically updated by the version control system with details of the change made.

A year later, when someone asks why systems are configured in a given way, the revision control system will show when the change in question was made. The comments in the revision control system point back to ticket 12345 in the ticketing system, which in turn shows the source of the request. The answer can be given: 'Joe Smith requested that the configuration be changed on ticket 12345 on 14th May last year. It was implemented by John, checked by Kate, and rolled out that evening'.

GETTING STARTED

There are lots of CMSs out there, with Wikipedia listing over 20 Open Source CMSs. The key players at the time of writing include:

- Ansible

- CFEngine

- Chef

- Puppet

- Salt

The implementation of a CMS is decidedly non-trivial. Whilst each of the systems listed above will have its pros and cons, broadly speaking they all do the same thing. Arguably more important than the system used is deciding how to organise the client systems into the right groups and/or hierarchy. In reality, both experience of a CMS and an understanding of your organisation are required. Here's how to get started:

- Define some requirements. What are the top five jobs you'd like to manage via a CMS? Look at the configuration language used by various CMSs: which fit your organisation best? How scalable do you need your CMS to be – will you be managing tens or hundreds of systems, or will it be several thousand?

- Pick a CMS that meets these requirements. The Wikipedia page (see *Resources*) is a good starting point.[6] Don't spend hours on this; just pick what appears to be the best for you right now.

- Start small. Set up one test client and use the CMS to carry out simple tasks (install a package, create a user, update a configuration file). Each 'simple' task will present challenges that need to be overcome.

- Get your 'top five' jobs implemented in a test environment.

- Add a 'real' server – perhaps a development or test machine – and run the CMS in 'dry run' mode on it. Examine the changes the CMS wants to make. Modify the CMS configuration if needed.

- Run the CMS for real on the development system and evaluate the results.

---

6   https://en.wikipedia.org/wiki/Comparison_of_open-source_configuration_management_software

You can continue in this way, gradually growing the number of clients and the reach of the CMS. You'll come across issues, of course, and you may realise that, with hindsight, some of your earlier decisions weren't the best. That's OK: you'll be on a learning curve to understand which is the right CMS and hierarchy for you. You may end up re-implementing almost from scratch. To quote Fred Brooks in his classic book *The Mythical Man-Month*, you should 'plan to throw one away because you will anyhow'.[7]

This example shows how one company radically streamlined its operations by using a CMS:

A high-tech chip design company has a need to employ a significant number of temporary engineering staff at various times during the design phase. Each of those staff need a Linux workstation, and require various utilities to be installed (editors, IDEs, compilers, debuggers, testing tools, and so on). They also need access to network resources, such as printers, code repositories, file servers, email, etc.

When such staff are employed, a workstation is built from scratch for them. The IT staff carry out a network (PXE) boot of the workstation and are prompted to provide two items of information: the machine's identity, and a confirmation that the disks should be overwritten. Once those are provided, the process of building the workstation

---

7   https://en.wikiquote.org/wiki/Fred_Brooks

is fully automated. The boot image installs Linux and the CMS client, and then the CMS client is run. Twenty minutes later, the workstation is fully built with all utilities, application programs, X windows, file shares, and so on. It only remains to reboot the workstation, and it's ready for use.

It's trivially easy to change the configuration of a new workstation: it's just a matter of editing files on the CMS server. Gone are the days of a 'gold' CD that would build a workstation, and which was complex and costly to maintain and update. The workstations are configured exactly as required, all are consistent, and 'it just works'.

GOTCHAS

It's not a perfect world, and whilst a CMS is an essential component of a Linux infrastructure, there are pitfalls. As discussed, a CMS is ideal for ensuring consistency across multiple servers, but in practice that means that any mistakes are consistent, too. There must a be a robust process whereby changes are both tested and reviewed before being deployed.

When the configuration of all of your servers is managed from one CMS system, you need to be certain that the CMS server is secure and that changes to that system are carefully managed. A compromise of the CMS server will allow a compromise of all the servers it manages.

Making major changes to how a CMS is implemented within an organisation is not trivial, and as the CMS embeds itself deeper into the infrastructure the change becomes harder still. A CMS is not alone in this respect, of course, but it can be deceptive: what starts as a mechanism to only ensure all necessary packages are installed on servers can quickly become something much more. There are three approaches that can help reduce the problem:

- Buy-in experience of implementing a CMS.

- Define clearly what you expect the CMS to achieve, and do not allow 'mission creep' to expand that remit without proper consideration.

- As already discussed, plan to throw one away anyway. The lessons learned will make the next implementation considerably better.

When should you start using a CMS? The glib answer is 'before you need one'. As soon as you have more than one server, you will benefit from a CMS in all the ways mentioned: consistency, an audit trail, reduced system management costs. It's unlikely that an organisation with two servers would be prepared to implement a CMS, but be aware that the phrase, 'If I knew then what I know now' may crop up in the future. Realistically, the best answer is 'sooner rather than later'. When IT staff are repeatedly logging in to systems to make the same changes, or when the irritation factor of different servers behaving in different ways starts to rear its head, that is the time.

SUMMARY

- Plan to use a CMS as soon as you have more than two or three servers

- Have a review process before rolling out changes via your CMS

- Ensure access to your CMS is secure

In this chapter, we've looked at the role of a CMS along with the pros and cons of using one. Although growing in popularity, CMSs are by no means ubiquitous, and they're often added as an afterthought. A better strategy is to use one as early as possible, and resolve to use it to implement *all* system changes.

CHAPTER TEN

Cloud Or Not?

Cloud technology has changed the face of server-based computing, but we should recognise that 'cloud computing' is an imprecise term. In general, when we talk about 'cloud computing' we are referring to services provided by the likes of Amazon Web Services (AWS), Google Cloud or Microsoft Azure. They provide effectively infinite compute resources in the form of virtual servers or *instances* together with high-level supporting services, such as databases, firewalls and load balancers. These components allow us to build a flexible, resilient virtual infrastructure. However, it's perfectly possible to use those same 'cloud' technologies in our own server room. At this point, relating a short history of how servers have been provisioned over time will help us determine how best to implement our planned Linux infrastructure.

A SHORT HISTORY OF SERVER CONFIGURATION

Prior to the mid-2000s, businesses would buy or lease hardware to run their applications. Those servers would be hosted either in a server room owned by the business or in a dedicated data centre, and each server would run multiple applications. Even relatively simple applications, such as a WordPress website, consist of multiple components. WordPress needs a web server of some kind (maybe Apache), a way of handling PHP code, and a database. So they'd build a server, set up Apache, PHP and a MySQL database, install WordPress and they'd have their company website live.

By and large, that worked. It worked well enough that there are still a huge number of servers configured in exactly that way today. But it wasn't perfect, and two of the bigger problems were *resilience* and *scalability*.

Lack of resilience meant that any significant issue on the server would result in a loss of service. Clearly a catastrophic hardware failure would mean no website, but there was also no room to carry out certain kinds of scheduled maintenance without impacting the website. Even installing a security update for Apache would necessitate restarting Apache, which in turn meant a (usually momentary) website outage.

The lack-of-resilience problem was largely solved by building 'high-availability clusters'. The principle was to have two or more servers running the website, and configured in such a way that the failure of any one server didn't result in the website being down. The *service* was resilient even if the *server* wasn't.

The scalability problem was a bit trickier. Let's say your WordPress site gets 1,000 visitors a month. One day, your business is mentioned on Radio 4 or breakfast TV. Suddenly, you get more than a month's worth of visitors in twenty minutes. We've all heard stories of websites 'crashing', and that's typically why: a lack of scalability.

The multiple servers that helped with resilience could be configured to share the workload amongst them. When all is well, two servers host your website, sharing the workload. Between them they could manage a higher workload than one server alone could – but this is still not ideal. You'd be paying for two servers 100% of the time, but for most of that time both would be working perfectly and it's likely that one alone could run your site. Then your business receives some good publicity, and you'd need ten servers to handle the load, but only for a day or two.

The better solution to both the resilience and scalability problem was cloud computing. Set up a server instance or two on AWS or Google Cloud, and if one of the instances failed for some reason, it could be restarted automatically. Set up autoscaling correctly, and when the workload on your web server instances rapidly rises additional server instances are started automatically to share the workload. Later, as interest dies down, those additional instances are stopped, and you only pay for what you use.

The cloud solution is much more flexible than the traditional standalone server, but it isn't the utopia it first seemed to be. Updating the running cloud instances is not straightforward. Developing for the cloud has challenges too: the laptop your developers are using may be similar to the cloud instance, but it is not the same. If you commit to AWS, migrating to Google Cloud is a non-trivial undertaking. And what if, for whatever reason, you simply don't want to hand over your computing to Amazon, Google or Microsoft?

SERVER CONFIGURATION TODAY

The contemporary solution is much smarter. The components of your application are decomposed into *microservices*: discrete units that provide just one service of the overall application, such as a database or a web server. Each microservice is run in a *container*, which is a self-contained software unit that can run anywhere: on AWS, on your own hardware, on Google Cloud, on your developer's laptop. If your developer is running OS X on her MacBook, you're running Windows on your office system, and your production system is running Linux, it still works. The container neither knows nor cares what operating system the hardware is running.

There are tools to help us build resilient, scalable and maintainable infrastructures that are not tied to a specific environment. One component is Docker, a mechanism for running the containers themselves, again in any environment from your laptop to AWS. Kubernetes is a *container orchestration* tool that can build and manage an infrastructure of containers. It will ensure sufficient containers are running, manage connectivity between them, load balance, manage container upgrades, and much more.

Kubernetes has its roots in Google, stemming from a Google project, GIFEE ('Google's Infrastructure For Everyone Else'). Google has been wildly successful running huge numbers of servers in a well-coordinated, secure way worldwide, and Kubernetes makes that technology available to everyone. Without doubt, Kubernetes is changing the face of big application computing.

Here's a quick summary of the pros and cons of each approach:

Standalone server pros:

- Simple and well understood
- Contained costs

Standalone server cons:

- Single point of failure
- No scalability
- Little resilience
- Greater administrative overhead

Traditional cloud infrastructure pros:

- Resilient
- Scalable
- Closely tied to provider

Traditional cloud infrastructure cons:

- System updates are complex
- Devolves some administrative overhead to the service provider

Container orchestration infrastructure pros:

- Resilient

- Scalable

- Provider agnostic

- Extremely flexible

- Built-in container management

Container orchestration infrastructure cons:

- Complex to implement

A note of caution: do not automatically associate cloud solutions with the big cloud providers. The technology used does not define where it runs: one of the benefits of containers is that they don't care whether they are running on hardware in your server room or running on AWS. The big cloud providers do have something of an advantage in the area of resilience by virtue of having multiple geographic *zones*, which means that even the failure of an entire data centre need not render your applications unavailable. However, all of the above can be implemented on your own premises and your own hardware if that is your preference.

So what's right for you? For any sizeable or complex infrastructure, it's hard to argue against a container orchestration system such as Kubernetes. The flexibility and built-in management are powerful arguments, and the truth is that in such an environment the underlying Linux environment is largely hidden. Developers can focus on writing, say, a Python 3.7 application and ignore how Python 3.7 is provisioned.

For more straightforward or modest infrastructures, the traditional cloud model can work well. The implementation needs to be specifically designed for such an environment – just replicating a standalone server will not give the best results – but the result can be an infrastructure that 'just works', with someone else worrying about hardware, environment, networking, and so on.

The attraction of a standalone server is fading. Its biggest advantage is tradition: such infrastructures have been around for decades and are well understood, familiar and comfortable. There are certainly some special cases where they will be the most effective – or even the only viable – solution, but for most new or developing infrastructures the other models are nearly always more appropriate.

SUMMARY

- Standalone servers are losing their appeal

- Simple solutions based on cloud technology can be very effective but need to be specifically designed for that environment

- Complex solutions are best served with a container orchestration system such as Kubernetes

In this chapter, we've looked at the options available for implementing our Linux infrastructure. We've started with the traditional standalone server, and discussed how its various shortcomings may be overcome. We've also looked at cloud infrastructures together with some of the issues they bring. Finally, we have looked at container orchestration systems, which bring the most flexibility at the cost of some complexity. If we plan on using an infrastructure provider such as AWS, we don't need to worry about how the underlying hardware is configured. However, for whatever reasons, it may be desirable to keep everything in-house or on premise, and to do that we'll need to build some servers.

CHAPTER ELEVEN

Server Design

In this chapter, we're going to focus on how to configure the hardware and low-level operating system upon which our Linux infrastructure will be built. If you're outsourcing the hardware provision to cloud suppliers, much of this will be taken care of by them.

SERVER CLASSES

A Linux infrastructure comprises servers, which we can split into the following broad classes:

Storage Servers focus on the safe, resilient and efficient storage of data. At the lowest level, there may be 'just a bunch of disks' (JBOD). As the name implies, this is just raw storage which can be handled by higher-level hardware. It's easy to expand: just add more disks or another disk expansion box. The next layer up will usually be a RAID controller, providing RAID management and data caching functions. It will present the RAID volume(s) to the operating system, which may carve them into Logical Volumes and even replicate them in near-real-time to another server to provide resilience in the case of hardware failure. Finally, at the top layer, the data will be made available to applications via a range of protocols – 'SMB' if Windows or Mac users need access, possibly NFS to make it available to other Linux systems.

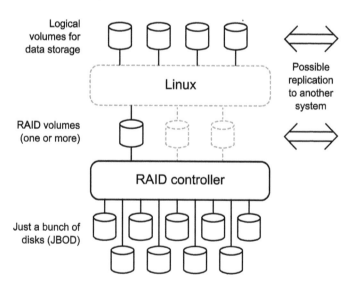

Storage server

Database Servers may host both relational (SQL) and non-relational (NoSQL) databases. For performance reasons, the database servers will typically manage their data storage. Database servers too may replicate data between themselves, and this is usually a function of the database software rather than a more conventional data copy process. The stored data is exposed via an Application Programming Interface (API).

Compute Servers typically take the data from a storage server, process it in some way, and then either present it to the user or store the modified data back on a storage server. For example, a web server may pull data from both a database server and a storage server, process it using some PHP or Python code, and present a web page to the user. Or, code may be pulled from a storage server, be compiled and have a regression test suite run against sample data, also from a storage server.

RESILIENCE

Underneath the covers, a server will consist of one or more power supplies, a motherboard, CPU(s), memory and storage; the basic components are the same as those of a desktop PC. The opportunity cost of server downtime is significantly higher than that of a PC, which leads to 'server' or 'enterprise' grade hardware being used for the server role. Server hardware typically includes:

- Multiple power supply units (PSUs). There are often two, although more may be used. The aim is to avoid a 'single point of failure' (SPOF). Tip: connect each power supply to an independent external feed, such as separate UPSs, to mitigate against supply failure.

- High-quality power supplies. The PSU has a greater impact on the day-to-day operation of a system than is generally appreciated. The role of a PSU is to convert mains-supply voltages to those needed by the internal components (typically 5v and 12v). The power demands from the rest of the system are not constant, and a measure of the quality of the PSU is its ability to maintain a constant output voltage as the current demand changes. A second measure of PSU quality is how 'smooth' the resulting DC voltages are. As well as converting voltages, the PSU takes incoming alternating current (AC) and converts it to direct current (DC). There will often be a 'ripple' on the output voltage showing echoes of the incoming AC current. Finally, PSUs do suffer from ageing, and in particular the smoothing capacitors can fail over time. A server-grade PSU will use higher-quality components than a consumer-grade PSU, providing a better-quality supply as well as a longer life.

- A server motherboard will often support multiple CPUs. It will also have some kind of 'out of band' (OOB) management interface, either built in or available as a plug-in extra, and exposed as an additional network interface on the system. Generically, they are 'intelligent platform management interface' (IPMI) connections, although individual manufacturers may have their own names for them, such as Dell offering DRACs (Dell Remote Access Controllers). The IPMI subsystem is an independent controller that allows monitoring and management of the rest of the server hardware. The exact features vary between implementations but often include:

  - monitoring of voltages, fans and temperatures

  - monitoring of hardware components (eg, a failed power supply)

  - an event log ('chassis opened' or 'memory error corrected', etc)

  - the ability to power on or off the main server

  - remote console, which can facilitate, for example, the installation of an operating system

- ECC (error correcting code) memory will be used. The nature of computer memory is such that corruption can (and does) occur, whereby a 0 bit becomes a 1 or vice versa. Lower-grade memory uses a *parity bit* to detect such corruption, but parity is limited to detecting so-called single-bit errors. If an even number of bits in one byte are flipped, parity won't detect that. Furthermore, even for single-bit errors, the error cannot be corrected, and all the memory can do is signal to the operating system that it has a 'memory parity error'. At this point, from the operating system's perspective, it cannot trust the memory at all, and the usual behaviour is to immediately stop ('crash'). By contrast, ECC memory can detect and correct single-bit errors, and it can detect (but not correct) double-bit errors.

- Enterprise-grade disks will be used, as discussed in Chapter 8. Even in servers that don't store much data, it is usual to build some kind of redundancy into the storage subsystem, such as the simple mirroring of two drives.

- Servers are typically packaged in a rack form factor, which allows efficient use of space. Rack mount servers will draw in air from the front to cool the server and expel warm exhaust from the rear. In order to maintain an appropriate environment, it is important that all servers are mounted round the same way, otherwise the warm exhaust from server A will be drawn in to server B. Any spaces in the rack should have blanking plates fitted to prevent the recirculation of warm air.

Many of the server features mentioned above – multiple power supplies, ECC memory, redundant disks – exist to mitigate the impact of some kind of failure. Effective monitoring of these servers is critical: if one disk in a RAID volume fails, you need to be aware of it so that corrective action may be taken. We'll discuss monitoring in detail in Chapter 13.

Redundant hardware alone won't prevent downtime. There's usually only one motherboard and one disk controller, and, whilst those components are extremely reliable, they can and do fail. One way of mitigating against catastrophic server failure is the high-availability cluster, mentioned in the previous chapter. Two or more servers work as one unit, and the resulting cluster uses sophisticated management software to monitor and manage two servers. As an example, let's assume that the service provided by this two-server cluster is a web server running on a typical 'LAMP' stack: Linux, Apache, MariaDB (or MySQL) and PHP (or Python). There are two major components: the database (MariaDB) and the web service (Apache). The management software will be configured using rules, and they might say:

1. One and only one instance of Apache *must* be running

2. One and only one instance of MariaDB *must* be running

3. Ideally, the Apache and the MariaDB processes will not run on the same system

Under normal circumstances, rule 1 will ensure that Apache is running on one server ('server A'), and rules 2 and 3 will ensure that MariaDB is running on the other ('server B'). Now imagine that server A, running Apache, fails. The management software notices that there is no longer an instance of Apache running, which contravenes rule 1. Because of rule 3, it will try to start Apache on server A, but will be unable to. It will then try to start it on server B and will presumably succeed.

The rules governing what runs where can be far more complex than the simple example given above. More importantly, for the usual case when both servers are functioning, the workload is shared between them, which will give better overall performance. It's also easy to migrate services between systems manually. If some work needs to be carried out on one server, the management software can be told to temporarily run both Apache and MariaDB on the other. Once the work has been completed, the configuration is returned to normal. The downside of this technique is that the initial set up and the ongoing management of the servers is complex.

SUMMARY

- Use enterprise-grade components in servers

- Use independent power sources for each server power supply

- Consider the use of clusters to mitigate against hardware failure

In this chapter, we've looked at the features of various hardware components that go into servers, together with techniques that can make the hardware more resilient against failure. For installations of more than a couple of servers, the container orchestration techniques discussed in the previous chapter will usually be preferred over standalone servers.

CHAPTER TWELVE

Backing Up Your Data

Things do go wrong from time to time, even in the most rigorous environments. The secret to surviving such events is preparation, and part of our preparation involves taking backups of our data. Backups serve two distinct purposes, and you should ensure that your backups are able to fulfil both – even if that means having multiple backups. The first purpose is the day-to-day backups, which exist primarily to account for human error and maybe the odd hardware failure, such as a document being accidentally deleted or Appendix A being inadvertently removed and a day's work is lost. These backups are usually made every night. If you didn't have this type of backup when needed then there would be frustration, irritation, maybe even the uttering of a particular word that succinctly summarises how you feel, but the document could be recreated. Your business would go on.

The day-to-day backups are often stored on site, in the same building as the original data. That's fine: having them locally means both the backup and any restoring process are much quicker. Those backups are for convenience, and anything that makes them more efficient to use makes sense.

The second purpose of backups is for disaster recovery. These are a different story; they exist to ensure the survival of the business. If you get to the office tomorrow and see only a smoking crater where your building used to be, the quality of the disaster recovery backups will play a very significant role in determining whether the business survives.

Before we get to the details of how backups should be implemented, let's spend a moment talking about copies of data that are *not* backups. These include:

- A database being replicated to a second system

- Data mirroring, such as that used in RAID disks

- Cloud data stores that replicate a directory to multiple devices

All of the above are useful and valuable techniques, and each helps mitigate against hardware failure, but none will protect you against human error because any changes to the source data are also propagated to the copy. When you delete a file from a mirror disk pair, it's removed from both disks. By contrast, a backup is independent of the data source.

There are three main options for backups: tape, local disk and online backups to a remote server. Tape is the traditional medium for storing backups, and as such its pros and cons are well understood. Its principal advantage is simplicity: a tape is a small, self-contained and relatively robust backup medium. However, the process of backing up via tape will always require some manual intervention. Any backup medium should be stored remotely from the server, which introduces another manual process in the use of tapes. If tapes are used, and if you have multiple tape drives that use the same media type, it is worth checking that a tape written by the first tape drive can be read by the second.

USB disks are cheap and easy to obtain, and it is relatively straightforward to carry out backups to them. Ideally, data will not simply be copied to a backup disk; rather, use a backup program that will catalogue which files are on each disk, and this will make restoring easier, too. However, there are significant disadvantages in using USB disks for backups. Disks are a lot more fragile than tapes, and dropping a disk will often make it unusable. They are also inherently less portable, and as such the human effort involved in moving them around will mean that they are less likely to be taken off site as a matter of routine. In the case of a disk backup that is 'taken home', there may well be security considerations, too. Finally, as with tapes, the process of backing up to disk will always require some manual intervention.

In reality, tapes and portable disks are rarely used as backup media today, with online backups being significantly more convenient. They are carried out using a secure, encrypted connection to another server, either local or remote, and offer the following advantages:

• They may be fully automated and thus not forgotten

• They require no manual intervention

• Successive revisions of files may be stored automatically, allowing a user to revert to an earlier version if required

• The integrity of the backup can be easily verified by examining the files on the backup server

• The status of the backups can be integrated into the server monitoring infrastructure

Online backups work by backing up only those parts of a data file that have changed. This means that the whole file need not be copied each time there is a change, which in turn results in quicker backups. The first backup, of course, requires that all the data be copied, which can be time consuming over a slower network link. It can be helpful to 'seed' the initial backup by temporarily placing the backup server on the same local network and carrying out one or two backups.

Data churn is the amount of data that changes between each backup, and it is a key factor in determining how long online backups take. It's relatively quick for a well-designed backup system to identify that a given file has *not* changed since the last backup and thus does not need to be copied again. That means that the majority of the time taken for the backup to complete is spent copying the files that *have* changed. A large, mostly static, data store is much quicker to back up than a smaller, frequently changing one. When the data churn is large enough that remote backups cannot complete in a reasonable time, it may be necessary to review what data is being backed up and even consider alternative ways of backing up that data.

There is a deep-rooted and fundamental difference between day-to-day backups and backups for disaster recovery, and it is essential that your backup regime recognises this fact. Disaster recovery backups differ from the day-to-day backups in that:

- They must be offsite
- They must prioritise business-critical data

That they must be offsite is, hopefully, self-evident. If your office has become a crater, it's unlikely that much in the way of on-site backups will have survived. The prioritisation of business-critical data is the part that is often not even considered.

In an ideal world, we'd be able to back up everything, every night, to an offsite backup, but sometimes the data churn, the network speed and the time available for backups conspire to make such backups unrealistic. That means you need to be selective in what is backed up offsite, but how do you determine what comprises the most important data? We turn to our Requirements Document. As discussed in Chapter 3, we identified some data as being business-critical, and that's where we start.

PUTTING IT INTO PRACTICE

The quantity of data that is truly business-critical will be a very small subset of your overall data. Step one is to identify that data and ensure it is being backed up off site at an appropriate interval.

The job isn't over once you've set the backups up. You need checks that run, automatically, every day to ensure that:

- The backup completed within a reasonable time

- There were no errors with the backup

- The last successful backup is recent (for example, within the last 36 hours)

Once the business-critical data is being backed up off site in this way, you can start backing up the business-operational data. You may subdivide this data into layers of importance, perhaps starting with financial data. The same criteria apply, and as there is now more data it will take longer to back up. As you add more layers, the time taken will increase, and you'll reach a point where either all data is being backed up in a timely way or you run out of time. Generally speaking, data backups take place overnight, and it's helpful for them to have completed (with some margin) before the business day begins. If you run out of time and you still don't have all your business-critical data backed up, you'll need to review how it is being backed up to find a faster way (or possibly reconsider what constitutes 'business-critical data').

Turning to the restoration of data from a backup, the secret of dealing with emergency situations competently and confidently is to practice them. On a modern airliner, engine failures are extremely rare: most pilots will go their entire career without experiencing one for real, but they practice them frequently. They practice them in a simulator, where making mistakes doesn't mean loss of an aircraft or loss of life. They hone their skills and, in some cases, the process itself, until both are as good as they can be. If they experience a real engine failure, such as the one on Thomson flight 253H, a well-rehearsed plan kicks in.

On 29 April 2007, a Boeing 757, Thomson flight 253H, started its take-off run at Manchester airport in the UK. Just as the aircraft was leaving the ground, a bird was ingested into the right engine, causing considerable damage. This is the most critical phase of the flight in which to have a problem: there's insufficient runway ahead to stop, so the crew are committed to take off, but now on only one engine. The crew executed a perfect take-off, engine shutdown and declaration of emergency, and 15 minutes later the aircraft landed back at Manchester. The entire incident was filmed (see *Resources*).[8] All those hours the pilots had spent practising engine failures in the simulator paid off: no one was hurt (well, except the bird), and – other than the engine – there was no damage to the aircraft.

Whilst backups may not be urgent, they are almost unparalleled in their importance in business. In the same way as the pilots hope never to experience a real engine failure, we hope we'll never have to use the offsite backups. If the engine does fail, we can be reasonably confident that the pilots can sort it out.

---

8   www.youtube.com/watch?v=9KhZwsYtNDE

How confident are you that your backups will be able to rescue the business?

The *only* way to know is to test them, and they should be tested by someone who has had no involvement in setting them up or managing them on a day-to-day basis. That means clear documentation is needed that doesn't make assumptions about the reader's knowledge. Skill level, maybe, but not knowledge: instructions such as 'log into the backup system' will need more detail ('by going to the following URL and logging in with the credentials stored at X'). Those instructions need to be stored off site, too, for obvious reasons. Keep a log of test restores from backups, noting when they were done, who did them, and what problems they had. If the person doing the restore cannot complete it without seeking help, the documentation is lacking – and that is very likely to be the case at first.

Despite agreeing with the principle of testing backups, precious few businesses actually do it. It is something that sits on the to-do list, and we'll get to it just as soon as we can. But you never know when you're going to need to recover from an emergency, and you seldom get any warning. The time to practice is now. Flying a Boeing 757 might be very different from managing a Linux infrastructure, but both demand professionalism. For an excellent demonstration of professionalism, go and watch (and listen to) that video of flight 253H linked to in the example above. Then schedule a practice emergency of your own: recovering data from a backup.

SUMMARY

- So far as possible, fully automate your backups

- Monitor your backups for errors, elapsed time and age

- Test your backups

One of the biggest problems with backups is that they are boring. We can all think of more interesting things to do than make a copy of some data – a copy that we'll almost certainly not need. So backups tend to get pushed down the priority list. Consequently, they get pushed to more junior staff, and the aim becomes merely to put a tick in the 'backups' box. 'We should probably improve our backups' is not an uncommon phrase to hear when reviewing an IT infrastructure.

As with so many aspects of a resilient IT infrastructure, proactive planning results in a more effective backup process. Unlike other aspects, however, we rarely see how effective our backups are unless we test them. You need to write and maintain a Backup Recovery Manual, and you need to ensure regular testing of restores from backups. It is critical that carrying out the schedule of test restores has the full backing of the senior management of the business.

CHAPTER THIRTEEN

Status Monitoring

Effective system monitoring improves both the
security and the availability of systems. Security
updates are released multiple times per week; being
aware of what security updates are outstanding
on your systems and taking steps to install them
will significantly improve your system security.
Similarly, being aware of potential problems before
they impact your business will improve availability. When you have multiple, redundant systems
or components, such as a fault-tolerant RAID disk
subsystem, you *must* monitor the health of the
individual components. The whole point of a fault-
tolerant system is that it continues to operate even
when parts of it fail. If you don't monitor it correctly,
you'll only become aware of failures when the entire
subsystem fails.

Monitoring can also maintain a historical record of problems. If you've determined that your systems must be available 99.99% of each month during the hours 08:00–20:00, a report from your monitoring system can show whether that's been achieved.

There are three types of monitoring to consider:

- Status monitoring

- Trend monitoring

- Log monitoring

In this chapter, we'll examine status monitoring, and in Chapter 14 we'll look at trend and log monitoring. The principle of status monitoring is simple: periodically – say every five minutes – the monitoring system connects to each of the client systems in turn and runs certain checks, usually with the aid of some locally-installed agent. The results of those checks are passed back to the monitoring server, which will typically:

- Record the data for later analysis if required

- Present the results of the tests, perhaps via a web page or other program

- Generate notifications as required

The monitoring server will usually also facilitate:

- Running single checks, or perhaps all checks for a specific client, on demand

- The creation of reports showing server or service availability statistics, periods of downtime, notifications issued, and so on

- Scheduling downtime for a host or service such that checks (and notifications) are suspended for a given period

- The acknowledgement of issues reported, which removes the issue from the main screen

- The recording of performance data – for example, CPU load

PARAMETERS

Most monitoring systems will monitor a wide range of parameters out of the box, including:

- Free partition space for every disk partition

- Validity of TLS/SSL certificates

- That specific applications are running

- Mounts of network disks

- Data replication status (databases, LDAP)

- UPS status

- RAID status

It's also possible to write custom checks to monitor additional parameters, which might be operational parameters or business-specific parameters. Such custom checks might include:

- Status of housekeeping tasks (database dumps, cron jobs, log rotation)

- Status of backups (age, errors, how long to run)

- Outstanding security updates to install

- Whether the 'orders' database table has had any rows added in the last ten minutes

Finally, it's possible to arrange for other processes to update the monitoring system asynchronously. For example, having the backup system notify the monitoring system of the status of the backups is more efficient than waiting for the monitoring server to check the backups. It also reduces the complexity of the monitoring system: rather than having it understand how to check backups, it simply reports what it has been told by the backup process. The goal should be to have only one place to go in order to review the status of the infrastructure. A mixture of 'status emails', log files and multiple 'dashboards', all reporting different elements of the infrastructure, is not nearly as helpful as One Place To Go For Everything.

The parameters you choose to monitor must satisfy two conditions:

- If unresolved, they will lead directly or indirectly to a problem for your business

- There is an identifiable action that can be taken when the parameters are reported as being outside the normal range

Let's consider some examples.

'Disk is 85% full'

Will this lead directly or indirectly to a problem for your business? If a disk (or disk partition) becomes full, that will undoubtedly affect the operation of that server, which will in turn impact the business. Monitoring the amount of disk space used meets the first criterion.

Is there an identifiable action that can be taken? Although the disk usage has increased, from below 85% to over it, which has triggered this warning, there isn't an immediate and urgent problem here. We still have 15% of disk space available, and the system will show no immediate problems as a direct result of a disk being 85% full. But there are things we can – and should – do. Our first action should be to find out where within the disk the majority of the space is being used, and see whether we can reduce that usage or move data elsewhere. We should also understand why the disk usage has increased.

We have satisfied both conditions: doing nothing will lead to a server outage, and there is a process we can follow to understand and remedy the problem.

'Backups are over twenty-four hours old'

Will this lead directly or indirectly to a problem for your business? The implication here is that the backups are not up to date. Indirectly, that is certainly a problem for the business if the backups are later required.

Is there an identifiable action that can be taken? Yes! Finding out why the backups have not run (or why the monitoring system thinks they have not run) should be a high priority. Once the problem is resolved, putting some thought into how the backup process could be made more resilient would be time well spent.

'High system load'

Will this lead directly or indirectly to a problem for your business? It's possible to measure the load on a Linux system, but that is a very crude indication of how busy a server is. However, the mere fact that a server is busy is not a problem in itself for the business – after all, the server is supposed to earn its keep, and – within reason – the busier it is, the more it is justifying its existence.

Is there an identifiable action that can be taken? An examination of the system will show which processes are using the most CPU time, but then what? Is it actually a problem that the database processes are using 68% of the CPU? And, if it is, what will we do about it?

System load may be of interest, but I'd argue that it isn't the right parameter to measure because, by itself, it's meaningless. It would be much better to monitor the rate at which work is being accomplished by the server, such as how long it takes for the overnight housekeeping tasks to run, or how long it takes for a web server to deliver one specific page.

TICKETING

The monitoring system may feed potential issues directly to the ticketing system, or it may simply alert the IT staff, who in turn raise a ticket manually as appropriate. Automatic ticket creation from the monitoring system is an attractive prospect, but it needs to be implemented with care to avoid a single but significant outage resulting in a plethora of tickets. For example, a network failure may make eight servers unreachable and cut off an even greater number of services, but it isn't helpful to have tickets created automatically for each and every service affected. To some extent, this may be mitigated by having service dependencies correctly configured (see below), but if you want to implement automatic ticket creation from the monitoring system, start with a small subset of detected issues and grow gently. If your monitoring system is customisable – and if it isn't, why not? – a compromise might be to put a 'create ticket' button on the web interface next to each issue reported. That can largely automate the creation of a new ticket, but only when manually triggered.

DEPENDENCIES AND NOTIFICATIONS

Some monitoring systems support the concept of dependencies, which allow us to define a dependent relationship between services. For example, some systems may be located at a remote site that is protected by a firewall. If that firewall fails, then the monitoring system won't be able to access any of the systems that it protects. Without dependencies, the monitoring system would report that all of them were down. We can define each of the remote systems as being dependent upon the firewall; now, if the firewall fails, the monitoring system will report its failure, but it will not create additional alerts for the now-unreachable systems behind the firewall.

The monitoring system should alert someone when it detects a potential problem, and that is the role of notifications. Notifications are typically very customisable and can take many forms, including:

- Email to one or more people

- SMS (text) messages

- Alert on web page

- Posting to IRC, Slack or some other chat system

- Creation of a problem ticket

- Audio alert

- Popup window

Notifications are limited only by imagination: if you can write a script to do it, the notification can trigger that script. Different notifications may be appropriate for different problem severity levels, different types of problems, problems that occur at different times, and according to who is being notified. For example, when a web page load time is too long, a ticket may be created and the support team leader notified during working hours. Outside of working hours, the ticket is still created but now a text message is sent to the on-call support team.

Escalations are a higher level of notifications. They typically occur when either a problem has not been acknowledged within a specific time or when an acknowledged problem has not been resolved within a specific time. The workflow might be:

- Critical problem detected: send notification

- Critical problem not acknowledged within 10 minutes: resend notification

- Critical problem not acknowledged within 15 minutes: send escalation

- Critical problem not resolved within 1 hour: send escalation

It's important to view the monitoring system primarily as an alerting tool rather than a diagnostic tool. Consider a check that retrieves a page from a remote web server and checks that the returned page contains a specific string that originated from a database on the web server. For this check to report 'OK', all of the following need to be working:

- DNS lookups on the monitoring server

- DNS entry for the web server

- Connectivity to the web server

- The web server software (eg, Apache) must be running

- Apache must accept a new connection

- The SSL certificate must be valid

- The web processing (eg, PHP) must be working

- The database software must be running

- The database must accept a connection from the web process

- The database lookup must succeed

- The page must be built and returned

- All of the above must happen within a reasonable time

If this check fails, it's unlikely to be immediately apparent where the problem is, but the aim here is to alert the support staff that something is wrong so that it can be investigated further.

Monitoring forty to sixty parameters per server is all very well, but what are you going to do when the monitoring system raises an alert? We'll discuss that in more detail in Chapter 17, but for now it's helpful to have documentation that:

- Lists every check that is run on any server

- Gives an overview of what each check does

- Gives advice about how to troubleshoot the system if each check fails

The more comprehensive this documentation, the more easily issues can be resolved. To put it another way, for an organisation with multiple IT staff members, good documentation in this area will help the problem to be resolved at a lower level.

MONITOR EXTERNALLY

It is important that the monitoring of publicly available services (eg, web and mail servers) is carried out outside of your infrastructure. A web server that is reachable from the adjacent server in the rack isn't necessarily reachable by users around the world.

External monitoring should also be applied to the monitoring server itself. If you're relying on the monitoring server to alert you to any issues, particularly outside of office hours, you need to have something that alerts you to the fact that your monitoring server has failed.

A few suggestions, based on experience:

- To identify systems within your monitoring systems, use Fully Qualified Domain Names (FQDNs). It might be tempting to name a server, from the monitoring perspective, 'Green web server' or 'Mail Server Newport'. Don't do it. 'Green web server' might be more appealing to the eye than 'webgreen.example.com', but when it comes to troubleshooting at 4am on a Sunday, the support staff will appreciate knowing exactly which server they should be investigating.

- Don't ignore problems on the main monitoring screen. The aim should be to have no unacknowledged alerts showing.

Ignoring one or more 'because we know about that' is a foolish strategy. If you know about it, acknowledge it or schedule downtime on that service (or just fix it!), but remove it from the monitoring screen.

- Don't use monitoring as a safety net. Don't rely on the monitoring system to alert you to a service that you know fails from time to time. The role of the monitoring system is to alert you to things you don't know about. If you have an ongoing intermittent problem, investigate it and resolve it before it develops into something more serious.

- Don't have a single check that replaces multiple smaller checks. It's possible to have one 'master' check that covers an entire server where, no matter what happens – /var at 85% full, backups failed, system clock more than 100mS out – this one check flags up the issue. Don't do that. If we acknowledge the one master check on example.com because the backup is over twenty-four hours old, we won't be notified of the disk failure that is later detected. Instead, have granular checks so that one problem being acknowledged does not have the propensity to mask a subsequent, unrelated problem.

SUMMARY

- Monitor your systems comprehensively

- Ensure there is action that you can take for every monitored parameter being out of bounds

- Have documentation that describes what is being checked and what to do if the monitoring detects a problem

Comprehensive system monitoring, together with the processes to use it effectively, is an essential and fundamental component of a resilient Linux infrastructure. It doesn't need to be perfect on day one: get something in place, and grow and develop it over time.

CHAPTER FOURTEEN

Trend And Log Monitoring

TREND MONITORING

Whereas status monitoring is helpful in identifying problems when they begin to make themselves apparent, system trend monitoring is concerned with looking at various system parameters over a longer period of time. Almost any parameter that lends itself to being plotted on a graph may be measured, and typically the following would be included:

- Disk space used

- Disk response time

- Memory usage

- CPU usage

- Network traffic

- Application performance data

It's not uncommon for around a hundred parameters to be graphed. Under normal circumstances, the trend graphs are not routinely examined, but there are occasions when they can be very helpful:

- Answering questions such as, 'How has the web server response time changed over the past six months?'

- Planning: every system, whether physical hardware or a virtual server, will be constrained by the weakest of CPU power, memory, disk throughput and network throughput. If you're planning to upgrade or replace a system, the trend graphs will help you identify which area of the server is the weakest.

- Reviewing the impact of code changes.

- Predicting when a system or system component will reach capacity.

- Identifying transient issues.

- System tuning.

Let's look at the last three in more detail.

Predictions

If our status monitoring reports that a disk partition has reached 80% capacity, it may be helpful to understand the rate at which it is filling. If we can graph disk space usage over time, we can see whether this is linear growth, in which case we can reasonably predict how long we have until the disk would be full, or whether there was a sudden change in the *rate* at which the partition is filling up, in which case it may be worth investigating what happened to cause the rate to change.

The graph below shows the disk usage of a system over time. It can be seen that the '/home' partition (the top line) was filling up between June and late September. The system status monitor alerted support staff to the fact that the disk was getting full, and the graph below enabled a judgement to be made that, unless something was done, the system would run out of space in about two months' time.
In this particular case, some files that were no longer required were deleted, shown by the drop in mid-October, but it would have been possible to schedule the fitting of an additional or larger disk if that had been appropriate.

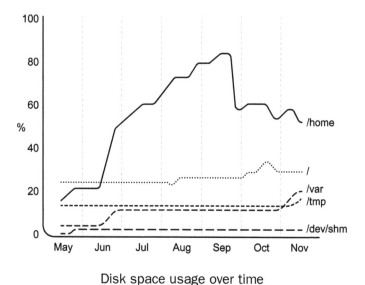

Disk space usage over time

Transient issues

Transient issues are those which disappear before a cause can be identified; for example, 'The web server was very slow yesterday around 2pm'. This statement is riddled with problems from a system administration perspective, which include:

- What does 'very slow' mean?

- Was it slow for everyone or just one user?

- What was the exact time when the issue began and ended?

Sometimes log files will show an obvious or possible cause, but failing that it can be hard to know where to start. Is this a database problem, a lack of memory, a network issue, more users than usual, or something else entirely? A look at the trend graphs for the time period in question can often give an indication. All we're looking for is a spike of some kind around 2pm yesterday. We might find, for example, that the number of database 'slow queries' peaked at 13:58. Why were there so many slow queries? It turns out that someone ran the end-of-month report during the day. Now we know why the website was slow, and to prevent the same problem happening next time we could:

- Improve the database indexing that the end-of-month report requires

- Prevent that report from being run during core business hours

- Automate generation and delivery of that report to the right people during the night

- Run the report against a read-only database replica on another system

- Have a monitor that measures website response times

System tuning

Effective system trend monitoring can also be used to improve system performance. If changes are made to system parameters with the aim of improving performance, a graph can readily show any change in performance with more conviction than a simple, 'it feels faster'.

It's possible to set up one server to hold the trend graphs for all systems; this has the advantage of reducing the workload on the remaining systems. The most demanding work is the rendering of the graphs themselves, which is typically carried out on demand rather than as a regular process, and a dedicated server means that additional load is not imposed on production systems.

LOG MONITORING

The final type of monitoring is log monitoring. The System Logger is an integral part of Linux and it keeps a record of things that happen on your server, such as:

- A user logs in
- A user runs (or attempts to run) a command with elevated privileges
- An email is received
- The internal clock is adjusted by 27 milliseconds
- An application creates a new customer record

For the most part, the examples given above are of little interest. However, when a user reports that they've not received an expected email, the logs allow the system administrator to check whether that mail has been received by the system and whether there were any problems with it (perhaps it was rejected because the recipient's address was mistyped).

Occasionally, there will be events logged that should be acted upon. Maybe a disk is reporting errors, or perhaps there are repeated attempts to log into a non-existent user account. The challenge is in finding the messages that are significant to your environment amongst the thousands of benign messages logged every day. Searching the logs manually is both time consuming and inefficient.

One approach is to define what log entries that require action look like, and have a report sent each time a match is found. The challenge here, though, is defining what to look for. Searching for 'error' in the logs might highlight some interesting entries, but it won't find a line reporting 'Unknown user: fredbloggs'.

A better approach is to do the opposite: define what we *don't* want know about, and then report on everything else. All of the same information is logged and available if required, but the report that is generated contains only what is left after the benign messages have been filtered out.

The aim here is to only ever receive reports that will be acted upon. If something is reported that does not require action, that 'something' should be added to the filters so it is no longer reported. Initially there's likely to be a lot of benign data reported, but over time such data can be filtered out and the reports become significantly more valuable.

The end result should be a small number of short reports detailing the log entries that didn't match the 'expected' ones, and which require action which, in turn, increases the security or availability or performance of your server. Once the reports are reduced to only those that require action, it is possible to feed the output of the log monitor directly into the status monitor, thus giving you one place to go for all non-trend monitoring information.

It's fair to say that setting up all the filtering to remove all the benign reports is a time-consuming process with moving targets. By contrast, trend monitoring is relatively simple to set up and, in my experience, more valuable.

SUMMARY

- Set up trend monitoring, even if it isn't routinely examined

- Use trend monitoring to measure the impact of system and application tuning

- Log monitoring is helpful, but less so than status and trend monitoring

In this chapter, we've looked at how trend monitoring is a useful resource to have, particularly when troubleshooting intermittent or poorly defined problems. Log monitoring can reveal useful data, but it is more challenging to set up and tune appropriately.

CHAPTER FIFTEEN

Documentation

Documentation: the bane of IT people everywhere. We all want perfect documentation so long as someone else writes it. Good documentation is the difference between a smooth-running, effective, consistent infrastructure and confusion. When the documentation is lacking or, worse, incorrect, the impact ripples outwards. Without clear, accurate documentation, there is more reliance on key personnel for their knowledge rather than their skill, and the same task will be performed differently depending upon who performs it.

There are a number of attributes a good documentation system must include:

- **Scalable**: The infrastructure is likely to grow over time, and the documentation system must be capable of scaling with it. The handy notebook might work when there are three people and one server, but it won't scale much beyond that.

- **Resilient**: Documentation needs to be backed up, which implies it should be online. Any edits must be made to the original; handwritten notes on a printout will not be there when the documentation is reprinted.

- **Secure**: As ever, security is a balancing act. We want our documentation to be kept up to date and to be accessible, but we need to control who may update it and possibly who may read it.

- **Accurate**: Out-of-date information within documentation not only leads to confusion; it also creates doubt as to the validity of the entire documentation. It should thus be everybody's responsibility to report or correct errors in documentation. Everything evolves, and this is no exception.

- **Accessible**: Documentation needs to be accessible in the sense of both knowing where to find it and being able to easily read and use it. There can be a tendency for some staff to keep private notes; that tendency should be discouraged. A private note suggests some lack of clarity in the documentation, and that should be resolved at source rather than each person having their own supplementary notes.

The days of written process manuals on the bookshelf are (or should be) long gone, and today a wiki is a simple, pragmatic and low-cost solution. There are many wiki implementations to choose from (see *Resources*),[9] but all allow pages to be edited in a web browser, usually by simply clicking on an 'Edit' button on the page. Whilst it is worth putting some thought into what features you require from a wiki before choosing one, don't make that process too long. Find one, implement it, start writing documentation. Review the use of the wiki after a few months, and if it transpires that it's too hard to use, explore alternatives in the light of experience. It's possible, although not always straightforward, to migrate from one wiki system to another. The danger in trying to find the 'perfect' wiki on day one is that no documentation is being written and maintained in the meantime, and without real-world experience it is difficult – if not impossible – to define the real requirements.

So, install a wiki, use it, fix it if it's broken.

---

9   https://en.wikipedia.org/wiki/Comparison_of_wiki_software

CHECKLISTS

Checklists are a hugely undervalued tool. They are used by pilots at every stage of a flight, and they are used by surgeons before carrying out an operation. It's no exaggeration to say that they save lives.

Within IT, they may not often save lives (although somewhere they will), but they act as a useful sanity check that all is in order. A checklist should not describe *how* to do something, merely that the current state is correct. If necessary, a checklist may refer to a process that holds more detail:

Data Centre Visit Checklist

- Access arranged with data centre (see Data Centre Access process)
- Access code for data centre
- Tools
- Laptop
- IEC to 13A adapter
- Photo ID

There can be resistance to the use of checklists. Some staff may feel they are above such things, relying on their experience to ensure 'everything is OK'. That's faulty thinking: arriving at the data centre only to be denied entry because you forgot your photo ID is annoying at best. A good checklist takes very little time to run through, but it can save lots of time later. It's also reassuring, as the surgeons were forced to admit:

When hospitals introduced checklists for operations, they too met with some resistance. Surgeons felt belittled by being asked to follow a checklist; some thought it an insult to their professionalism. However, when asked whether, if they were the patient, they would like *their* surgeon to use a checklist, the response was a resounding 'yes'!

As human beings, we have a greater-than-justified confidence in our own infallibility.

How the checklists are implemented is not important. A list on a page in a wiki; a printed, ticked and signed sheet; project management software – any of these options is fine. Use what works – and what your staff will be willing to use – in your environment.

One particular type of check we favour at Tiger Computing is the 'independent check'. Originating in the aviation industry, the independent check is carried out by someone who has not been involved with the work to date. They're typically used when the cost of missing something on the checklist is high. In the aviation industry, a second engineer will inspect the work after completion to ensure that the assembly is correct, the locking wire is in place, the cables are connected correctly, the tools removed, and so on. In the IT world, you might employ an independent check after security-sensitive work, such as the process to follow when someone leaves the business.

Like all documentation, checklists are not static. Arriving at the data centre and discovering that the keys to the rack are on your desk back in the office means that either the checklist is broken (you need to add 'Rack keys' to it) or it wasn't followed.

SUMMARY

- Implement a wiki to start organising your documentation

- It should be a requirement for everyone to keep documentation accurate and complete

- Make liberal use of checklists

Robust documentation is an integral part of managing IT. Getting started need not be hard. A wiki can be installed and operational in under a day. If you want to get started right now (and if not now, when?), get MediaWiki installed. That's the same software that Wikipedia uses. It may turn out, in the fullness of time, that you decide to change the wiki software you use, but in the meantime you can start building up your documentation.

SECTION THREE

SUPPORT

Now that we have specified and built our infrastructure, we need to keep it running. The principles of this section are very simple:

- We define a series of processes that ensure that the infrastructure continues to meet the defined requirements

- We ensure that staff have access to, are trained in and understand those processes

Having the processes defined in writing brings a number of advantages:

- Joined-up thinking: The act of defining the processes forces us to think through different scenarios and will, in itself, result in better integrated operations.

- Consistency: There's frequently more than one way to do it. When processes are defined, everyone knows 'how we do things around here'. When a problem arises, we don't have to spend time investigating how things were set up – we know.

- Training: Whilst sitting someone down in front the documentation may not be the best way to train people, it is a solid reference upon which appropriate training can be built.

- Efficiency: Well-defined processes will take into account how different parts of the IT support operation interact, and also how the IT department interacts with the rest of the business.

- Evolution: The feedback of experience allows us to improve processes over time. They need to be in writing so that all may benefit from those improvements.

The processes are in place so that as various incidents, problems and requests arise they are dealt with in an appropriate manner. If they are not dealt with appropriately, it will be for one of two reasons:

- The process is deficient in some way

- The process isn't being followed correctly

This greatly simplifies the day-to-day management of the infrastructure, and, if things do go wrong, it's relatively straightforward to identify where changes need to be made to prevent a recurrence.

It's not uncommon for the support function to be partially or completely outsourced to a third party. However, even if that is your intention, it's useful to understand how support functions for a couple of reasons:

- You will need to interface with it.
  Understanding the other side of that interface, and some of its challenges, will make that easier

- Being familiar with support best practices will help when selecting a partner to outsource to.

Let's take a look at support.

CHAPTER SIXTEEN

Ticketing Systems

The idea of a ticketing system is not new. We've all sent emails to a helpdesk and received an automated reply telling us that our reference number is 171117-001113. Welcome to ticketing systems.

There are two primary roles of a ticketing system:

- Task management for a helpdesk

- To maintain a historical record of work done

Tickets originate from a variety of sources: a user reporting a problem by telephone or email, an automatically-generated periodic ticket, a new user request, and so on.

TICKET STATUSES

Tickets pass through three fundamental stages: pending, being worked on and complete; however, a good ticketing system will allow a greater granularity. Here's an example of the various stages or statuses a ticket may have:

New: a ticket that has been created but has not yet been investigated

Open: a ticket that is being, or is ready to be, actively worked on

Stalled: a ticket that is waiting for a response from a third party, often the user who raised the ticket. For example, the support staff may have updated the ticket to request more information, and the ticket is then stalled awaiting the reply. Tip: It's possible for tickets to remain in a stalled state for a long time, so it's worth considering some kind of process to review stalled tickets after a certain time.

Autoclose: This is similar to 'Stalled', above, but after a predetermined time (for example, three working days) the ticket is automatically marked as resolved. A polite support desk will tell users that they believe the issue is resolved and ask whether the user is happy to close the ticket. Human nature being what it is, if everything is working correctly the user will often not reply. The 'Autoclose' status gives them time to reply. If they do, the ticket status changes back to 'Open'; if no reply is forthcoming, the ticket closes automatically.

Rejected: This status may be used to mark spam or tickets created in error; it indicates that the ticket will not be progressed.

Resolved: The original problem has now been resolved, and no further action is planned.

For some organisations, a 'two-stage close' is appropriate. Once a ticket is marked as 'Resolved', it is put into a queue to be reviewed by the support manager or other senior staff. Once reviewed, the ticket is either reopened, if more work is appropriate, or it is marked 'Closed'. This technique can be useful when new members of staff are on board, allowing a check to be made of how well they are handling tickets and communicating with users.

TICKET WORKFLOW

Here's a typical helpdesk workflow:

- An event occurs. A user can't log on, a new piece of software needs to be installed, a security certificate will expire soon, or a routine review and update of the Disaster Recovery plan is due.

- A ticket is raised.

- The ticket is assessed and given a priority and maybe a category, and it is usually put in a queue to be dealt with. In the case of a high-priority ticket, it may be given directly to someone to work on.

- One of the support staff takes the ticket and works on it. There may be escalations involved within the support team, but ultimately it will be resolved one way or another.

- Confirmation is sought from the original requester that the ticket may be closed.

All tickets are not equal, so, as in the third point above, we need to classify them. When a patient visits the Accident and Emergency department of a hospital, one of the first things that happens is they see the *triage* nurse. The role of the triage nurse is to determine the urgency of treatment appropriate for this patient. Patients presenting chest pain and shortness of breath are likely to be seen by a doctor before someone who has cut their finger.

We can take the principle of triage and apply it to our incoming tickets. The aims of the triage process are to:

- Ensure events are recorded by the creation of a ticket. Some events may already be ticketed – for example, a user may send an email to the helpdesk, which automatically creates a ticket – but other events, such as a user contacting the helpdesk by telephone, will require a ticket to be created manually. A copy of the ticket should always be sent to the requester.

- Determine the initial priority of tickets, which will usually be based upon the SLA. The user may indicate a suggested (or requested) priority, but ultimately this should be set by the helpdesk.

- Classify the ticket as an *Incident*, *Problem* or *Request*. This is discussed in the next chapter.

- Provide an initial response to the user in the case of user-raised tickets. Although most ticketing systems will send an automated reply to new tickets, a human reply, ideally giving some indication of when the ticket will be investigated, can significantly improve the helpdesk-user relationship.

The triage role is not an overtly technical one, and it can be performed effectively by junior technical staff or even non-technical staff.

Some tickets may require different skill sets or different levels of expertise, and a good ticketing system will help with matching tickets to an appropriately skilled person or team. Ticketing systems often allow arbitrary 'queues' of tickets.

It's worth considering how all these elements – statuses, priority, queues, and so on – will fit together.

Each member of the support team must be able to easily identify the next ticket that they should work on. You do not want staff cherry-picking tickets: they should follow a process. Whether a new, high-priority ticket should be handled before a lower-priority but older ticket is determined by the process. You may have one queue of tickets that are sorted according to your process, and from which all support staff work, each simply taking the top ticket. You may decide to have multiple 'feeder' queues for different staff skills or levels; however, a note of caution. Multiple queues will be handled at different rates, and it becomes harder to ensure that the *right* ticket is worked on next. I'd recommend one feeder queue, which may have complex sorting logic, so that it becomes easier for the staff to take the right ticket to work on next without having to think about it.

How the ticketing system is managed will depend to a large extent on how many tickets are open at any one time and how many IT staff there are. At the simplest level, having a screen display all open tickets is sufficient. However, that quickly becomes unmanageable as the number of tickets and staff grows. One approach is to have a 'dashboard' that shows:

- Any tickets that are scheduled to begin being worked on in the next twenty-four hours. This is specifically for tickets with an agreed start time; for example, the work may necessitate system downtime at an agreed time.

- All active Incidents.

- Any tickets flagged by support staff as requiring special attention.

- Open Requests.

- How many tickets each person has been assigned.

- The age of the oldest ticket.

- Whether high-priority tickets are getting dealt with.

The value of being able to access the ticketing system via an Application Programming Interface (API) should not be underestimated. Running nightly queries and building graphs showing statistics such as the number of open tickets can be valuable in measuring the efficiency of the helpdesk.

SUMMARY

- Mandate that all work done by the helpdesk is recorded in a ticket

- Implement a triage system to reduce the workload on more senior staff

- Monitor the number of tickets in each state and ensure tickets are moving through the system

The ticketing system is the heart of the day-to-day operations of an IT department. When set up well, it will greatly ease the day-to-day management of the support department. Expect the ticketing system to evolve over time, but bear in mind that it must remain usable. To paraphrase a quote often attributed to Albert Einstein, keep it as simple as possible but no simpler.

CHAPTER SEVENTEEN

Incidents, Problems And Requests

In this chapter, we'll look at one way of classifying tickets that can be used as a basis for implementing ticket management within your organisation. Some of the principles are derived from the Information Technology Infrastructure Library (ITIL). ITIL defines in some detail sets of processes and procedures that may be used to implement IT services management. It was originally developed by the UK Government's Central Computer and Telecommunications Agency (CCTA), and is now jointly owned by the UK Government and Capita plc.

ITIL categorises tickets as *Incidents*, *Requests* or *Problems*.

An **incident** is defined by ITIL as:

> 'An unplanned interruption to an IT service or a reduction in the quality of an IT service. Failure of a configuration item that has not yet impacted service is also an incident. For example, failure of one disk from a mirror set.'[10]

ISO 20000-1:2011 defines an incident (part 1, 3.10) as:

> 'unplanned interruption to a service, a reduction in the quality of a service or an event that has not yet impacted the service to the customer'.[11]

Examples:

- A web page displays errors

- A user cannot log in

- A server will not power up

- A disk is becoming full

The first three are easy to understand, and may be summed up by 'Something that was working yesterday is not working today'. The last, the disk filling up, is covered by the part of the ISO20000 definition that states, '...an event that has not yet impacted the service to the customer...'. In other words, we don't need to wait until the disk is full before we have an

---

10   https://en.wikipedia.org/wiki/Incident_management_(ITSM)
11   Ibid.

Incident: merely having it more full than some pre-determined level is sufficient.

Requests, or more correctly *change requests*, are often driven by users. Examples:

- The creation of a new user account
- The installation of a software package
- The retirement of a server
- Difficulty in carrying out a task

Again, the first three are easy to understand, but care must be taken with the fourth. This may be due to an underlying issue within the Linux infrastructure, in which case this ticket should be recategorised as an Incident, or it could be a user training issue. Supporting *users* should be differentiated from supporting the *infrastructure*.

In contrast to Incidents, a **Problem** may be defined as 'a condition often identified as a result of multiple incidents that exhibit common symptoms' (courtesy of the CCTA).[12] Problems are almost always raised by the IT staff themselves rather than users or some external agency. Examples:

---

12 https://en.wikipedia.org/wiki/ITIL#Problem_management

- Three disks have failed in server X in the past four months

- Backups of server Y fail for no obvious reason about once a week

- A service failure on server Z wasn't detected by the monitoring system

The third example above should be recorded as two tickets: an Incident regarding the service failure itself, and a Problem regarding the fact that the monitoring system didn't detect the service failure. Whereas Incidents represent issues affecting services, Problems represent issues that are likely to give rise to Incidents in the future. Identifying and resolving Problems leads to fewer Incidents, which in turn leads to more reliable systems.

A common approach is to assign tickets to a support 'level'. Level 1 tickets can be resolved by following established, documented processes, such as the creation or deactivation of a user account. Level 1 staff may also add more relevant detail or context to more complex tickets that may ultimately not be resolved by staff at that level. When a ticket cannot be fully resolved by Level 1 staff, it should be escalated to Level 2.

Level 2 staff will be more experienced and are capable of investigating issues on their own initiative. There may be guidelines in place as to how much time may be spent on each ticket before it is reviewed by more senior staff. Only exceptional tickets should be escalated to Level 3, and a note should be added to the ticket explaining why that escalation has taken place. Level 3 staff will be the most experienced and most qualified staff. They will typically be dealing with infrastructure problems, recurring issues, technically complex projects, and the like.

The aim should be to resolve all tickets within the time defined by the SLA and at the lowest level possible. For Level 2 staff in particular, they will sometimes be prevented from progressing the ticket through to resolution by a lack knowledge in one area. Rather than escalate the ticket to Level 3, a useful technique can be to flag the ticket for 'surgery'. One or more of the Level 3 staff will hold a 'surgery session', perhaps each morning and each afternoon, when such tickets are reviewed and some assistance or advice is given to the Level 2 staff to allow them to progress the ticket. This kind of arrangement both grows the skill set of the Level 2 staff and reduces interruptions to the Level 3 staff.

TICKET RESOLUTION

Print this out in large letters and hang it on the wall where your support team sit:

Our job is to fix customers, not systems.

It may be that, in the process of fixing a customer, we need to fix a system or two, but the focus should be on the customer. The customer may be an external fare-paying customer in the traditional sense, or they may an 'internal customer' who works for the same business.

With that focus in mind, a number of points emerge:

- Assigning support staff targets in terms of the number of tickets they must resolve is often counterproductive. It's easy to close tickets, but that doesn't mean that the user is happy, or even that the problem is resolved.

- When it is thought that the problem is resolved, asking the customer if they are happy for the ticket to be closed is a good way to improve customer satisfaction. Sometimes when the problem is fixed, the customer won't reply to such a question, so it's reasonable to assume after, say, three days that the ticket may be closed.

- New or less experienced staff may be prevented from resolving tickets, instead passing them to a team leader or manager for review. That helps ensure that new staff are following the correct processes and are keeping customers informed.

INTEGRATED WORKFLOW

There are three key systems involved in managing and maintaining an IT infrastructure: the monitoring system, the ticketing system, and the configuration management system (CMS). There will be other supporting systems, such as code repositories and documentation, but the principal systems are those listed above. Using them together in harmony can be beneficial, so let's look at how that may be achieved.

There are fundamentally two types of tickets: infrastructure failures, represented by Incidents and Problems, and infrastructure changes, represented by Requests.

Consider an example of the first ticket type, wherein the monitoring system reports that a disk on web1. example.com is 85% full:

- The monitoring system initially identifies the problem.

- Either the duty triage person or the monitoring system creates a ticket. The ticket subject will be something like, 'web1.example.com:/var 85% full', and for some reports the body of the ticket may hold more data.

- On the monitoring system, the problem is 'acknowledged' with a comment giving the ticket reference, such as '#27119: web1.example.com:/var 85% full'. The acknowledgement starts an audit trail by linking the problem reported by the monitoring system to the ticket.

- The ticket is classified, in this case as an Incident as it has the potential to impact services, and is fleshed out as required. It may be given a priority, there may be a department name or customer name to include, and so on.

- Supporting evidence and information is gathered if required. It may be appropriate to attach a graph of the /var partition usage over the past twelve months from the monitoring system so that the growth rate may be analysed.

- The ticket is placed in a queue to be looked at, initially by a Level 1 person.

- Upon resolution, the ticket is updated (What was the cause? What was the fix?) and either closed or passed to senior staff for review.

An example of a Request ticket would be one from a developer to install the Emacs editor on both of the development servers. Here's the flow:

- The developer emails the support desk with his request, which automatically creates a ticket and sends him an acknowledgement.

- The triage person classifies this ticket as a Request, and – as above – details, such as the priority, are established. Part of this process may be checking that the developer is authorised to make such requests.

- The ticket is placed in a queue to be looked at in turn.

- The support staff person taking the ticket will most likely propose a change to the CMS that will install Emacs on the appropriate servers. The necessary change will be made within a source code control system, such as Git, and a 'merge request' will be issued to move the change into production.

- Once the proposed changes are in place, the ticket is passed to another support team member for checking. Being able to control the configuration of multiple systems from a CMS is a huge benefit, but there's also the propensity to cause a lot of damage if care isn't taken; hence the independent check. If the change is approved, it is merged into the live CMS configuration, and ideally the source code control system will automatically update the ticket. If the change is not approved, the ticket is passed back for refinement.

The end result is that we can clearly see who requested the change, who implemented it and who signed it off.

SUMMARY

- Categorise tickets as Incidents, Requests or Problems

- Implementing support levels is helpful when there are more than a couple of support staff

- Cross reference between the various support systems (ticketing, configuration management, documentation, etc)

IT support sometimes gets bad press within businesses, and equally there can be some disdain within the support team for the non-IT staff of the business. Part of the problem is often communication: the IT staff are frustrated because the user's report isn't clear, and the user is frustrated because the problem hasn't been resolved. So, help the non-IT staff report problems in a way that expedites their resolution. There's a 'How To Report IT Problems' page on the Tiger Computing website (see the *Resources* page). You may want to take the ideas there and use them within your business.

The handling of tickets is the day-to-day bread and butter of an IT department. Inevitably the processes and policies will evolve over time, but keep your eye on the real goal: the job is to fix customers, not systems.

CHAPTER EIGHTEEN

Desktop Systems

Throughout this book we've considered Linux on servers, but most users don't log in directly to servers. In this chapter, we'll look at why users shouldn't log in directly to servers, how workstation support differs from server support, and how workstations can best be managed. Although I'll refer to 'workstation' systems, the same considerations apply to any user device – desktop, laptop, tablet, phone.

There's usually nothing to prevent users logging in directly to a server, but it's often inconvenient. Many Linux distributions will not install a graphical environment by default on a server, and that's a good thing. No graphical environment means less software installed, which reduces the so-called 'attack surface' for vulnerabilities. Graphical environments place demands on CPU and memory, which may be better used by the core functions of the server. There's also no need for many user-level programs to be installed on a server. Finally, the user will need to log in from somewhere, so some kind of user-level device will be needed anyway. On that note, users should never be allowed to log in at the system console, or even have access to it. A sufficiently knowledgeable user can bypass almost all security measures if they have access to the console.

It's important to differentiate between *user support* and *system support*. User support is more often concerned with how to use applications, whereas system support is about monitoring, maintaining and evolving systems. Our concern here is system support.

Support of workstations can be very simple if a few guidelines are followed. The first is that no business-critical data should be stored on workstation systems. Data – a document, some source code – may be copied to a workstation system to be worked on, but the workstation system must not be the primary store for that data. This immediately gives a number of major benefits:

- Workstation systems don't need to be backed up

- Workstation systems don't need hardware redundancy (RAID disks, multiple power supplies, and so on)

- Workstation systems can be quickly replaced in the event of a problem

The support process for a workstation could be to spend up to thirty minutes trying to resolve the problem and, if that is unsuccessful, to then rebuild the workstation. The rebuild should be quick and straightforward if workstation builds are managed by your Configuration Management Server. If you have a spare, ready-built workstation available, one of those can be used by the affected user and the impact of the problem is reduced still further.

Whilst clean and simple, there are a couple of potential issues with this approach. The first is that, despite any policy to the contrary, users may still store the only available copy of business data on their workstations. If the workstation fails or is rebuilt, that data may be lost. The second is that users will have some personal data they want to retain, such as browser bookmarks, working environment customisations and maybe some smaller documents that are in an embryonic stage. There are two solutions to these issues:

- Back up the workstations anyway. This only needs be a local backup; workstation-only data should rarely, if ever, be backed up remotely. The disadvantage of this approach is that, if a workstation is rebuilt to resolve an issue (or a spare workstation is used), there is a data restoration step to take as well.

- Store users' 'home' directories on a server. This gives true workstation independence, but the downsides are that more server storage space is required, there will be more network traffic and accessing data stored on a server will always be slower than locally stored data.

The speed of accessing a server-hosted home directory is more of a problem in certain environments. A user who updates a few documents or spreadsheets may not have a problem, but a software engineer who is compiling code may find that the number of files that have to be read and written over the network has a significant impact on performance. As the number of users grows, the demands on both the network and the server – both processing power and disk space – will also grow, making this approach harder to scale well.

One middle-ground approach is to use a file hosting and synchronisation service. Dropbox and Google Drive are amongst the better-known commercial offerings, but there are Open Source alternatives, such as ownCloud or Nextcloud, that may be installed on local servers. These utilities offer a range of services, but at their core they keep a local disk directory synchronised with a master directory on the server. Any changes made locally are propagated to the server copy, which in turn can propagate them to other devices – office workstation, home workstation, etc. Significant advantages of this approach include:

- The file synchronisation is asynchronous. It happens in the background and users don't have to wait for it (indeed, they can largely ignore it altogether).

- It's automated. Changes to files, new file creation and file deletion are automatically propagated.

- It's both more secure and more convenient than users copying files to a USB stick to work on elsewhere.

- Access to the server file store can be exposed via a web interface, making the files available anywhere if required.

- Many such services retain older copies of files for a time, often configurable, giving users the opportunity to roll back to an older (or 'deleted') version of a file.

Not every workstation directory should be mirrored in this way, and it works far better – and is the default –

for a subdirectory of a user's home directory to be mirrored. As an example, ownCloud creates and synchronises a directory called 'ownCloud' under the user's home directory.

SUMMARY

- Differentiate between workstation support and user support

- Consider local (-only) backups for workstations

- Consider the use of ownCloud or Nextcloud

Interoperability between Linux servers and non-Linux devices is very good. There's no reason why users can't have a Windows or OS X desktop system and use Linux servers at the back end. Regardless of platform, the same user support principles apply. Key to providing an appropriate level of support to users is distinguishing between user support and device support.

CHAPTER NINETEEN

Software Updates

Software updates take two forms. The first is enhancements: a new release of an application with new features. However, alongside the new and desirable features may be changes in how the application works that are not so desirable, and those may necessitate additional user training or changes in how the application interacts with other parts of the business.

The second form of updates is bug fixing. The present state of software engineering techniques means that our software has bugs, which are predominantly revealed by testing or using the software. There are many types of bugs, but the types that concern us here relate to security, usually in the form of either information exposure or allowing a non-privileged user to gain elevated privileges. When bugs are revealed after the software has shipped, an update may be released to address the vulnerability. In order to keep our systems and data secure, we need to ensure that such security updates are installed in a timely manner.

COMMON VULNERABILITIES AND EXPOSURES

When a security flaw is discovered, it is disclosed to a restricted list of interested parties. A fix is devised, often by the software author or by one or more of the Linux distributors, and that fix is released. Part of the aim of the limited disclosure is to help all distributions release the fix at around the same time.

Vulnerabilities are identified by a 'CVE' number, which is a reference to the Common Vulnerabilities and Exposures database. This system is managed by the not-for-profit MITRE Corporation, funded by the US government, and lists publicly declared vulnerabilities and exposures in publicly released software, including beta and other test versions. It's an easy way of unambiguously referring to a particular vulnerability.

The major Linux distributions maintain their own databases that show which version (if any) of a given package resolves a given CVE number. Let's consider an example: you have a web server that is running Apache 2.4.25, which is vulnerable to CVE-2011-4415. If you want to know more about this vulnerability, you locate it up in the CVE database.[13] That gives a brief summary, but if you wanted more detail still, you could follow the link to the National Vulnerability Database,[14] which gives more technical detail and also assesses the risk ('LOW') and the impact ('Allows disruption of service'). You're running Debian, so you go to the Debian Security Bug tracker,[15] and enter 'CVE-2011-4415' in the search box. The resulting page tells you that that vulnerability is fixed in Apache version 2.4.25-3+deb9u4, so, as long as you're running that version or later, your system isn't vulnerable to that bug (all of the links quoted in this paragraph are on the *Resources* page).

SECURITY UPDATES

Some Linux distributions are very disciplined about exactly what is included in a security patch. For example, when Debian releases a security fix it includes only that security fix. It won't include any new functionality or even non-security bugfixes. At any given time, the current release of the Debian

---

13 https://cve.mitre.org/cgi-bin/cvename.cgi?name=CVE-2011-4415
14 https://nvd.nist.gov/vuln/detail/CVE-2011-4415
15 https://security-tracker.debian.org/tracker

distribution contains tens of thousands of software packages that have been tested together, and introducing changes to those packages may compromise that interoperability. There are mechanisms for releasing new functionality into a subset of packages, but they fall outside the realm of security updates and require explicit action on behalf of the system administrator.

The 'only releasing security updates' philosophy is sound, but it can introduce a problem if your systems are externally scanned for vulnerabilities. Let's suppose the (fictitious) superweb server package is at version 1.2 and a vulnerability is discovered. The author resolves that vulnerability in version 1.3 but also includes a minor fix to another non-security issue. The distributions that are strict about only including security patches in security updates will not want to release version 1.3 as part of their current stable release. Instead, they will take the security patch element only and apply it to 1.2. They can't package that as version 1.2 or 1.3 because it doesn't actually match either, so they package it as something like 1.2-1.

Some external security scanners will only look at the version of the software that is installed, not whether it is actually vulnerable. They know that vulnerabilities exist in versions prior to 1.3, so when they see a version of 1.2-1 they incorrectly report a security failure. If this happens, the failure will usually be reported as vulnerable to a given CVE. You can use that CVE number to check with your distribution's security database, find that it's fixed in 1.2-1 and later, and thus verify whether or not your system actually is vulnerable.

The installation of most security updates is very straightforward, although updates to services (databases, web servers, etc) will usually involve a restart of that service to pick up the updated version. That usually results in the non-availability of that service for a couple of seconds, and for that reason installing security updates outside of key business hours may be desirable.

Kernel security updates are not so trivial. In order to make the new kernel live, a reboot will usually be necessary. That means a few minutes of downtime, and it involves a slightly higher risk than the more run-of-the-mill updates. An evaluation of the risks and benefits of updating the kernel can be carried out, and deferring some kernel updates may be appropriate.

APPLICATION INSTALLATION

Where possible, the best solution by far is to install the applications from the Linux distribution repositories, which brings a number of advantages:

- Ease of installation: One command takes care of everything, including installing any documentation and configuration files. This process can easily be performed by the CMS.

- Dependency management: The application package will detail all of the dependent software that is needed to run the application (library packages, other utilities, and so on).

- Consistency: The same package will be installed and configured in the same way everywhere.

- Rollback: If necessary, a rollback to a previous version of the package is relatively straightforward to achieve.

- Resilience: The installation process will be well tested, both by the Linux distribution itself and countless users.

- Updates: If a vulnerability is fixed in the application itself or any of the dependent packages, the Linux distribution security team will usually roll out an update quickly. That can be installed as part of normal operations, thus keeping the application secure.

- Upgrades and removals: The distribution package management tools know how to upgrade a package in place. They also know how to remove all elements of a package cleanly. Dependent packages, such as libraries, can be automatically removed if no other packages depend on them.

All the above applies to software packages that are part of the current version of the Linux distribution in use. From time to time, it may be considered desirable to run software that is not available in that distribution. It may be that a later version of the software is required, or it may be that the required software isn't packaged for your distribution at all. There are a number of options.

The first is to install the required package from a later version of your chosen distribution, although that won't always be possible. Some distributions make this easier than others. Debian, for example, supports a 'backports' repository, which contains versions of software that will appear in the next stable release of Debian but which have been repackaged for the current stable release. They won't be as well tested, but if you must use versions that are not currently packaged for your release the backports repository is usually your best bet. Red Hat systems can be similarly updated with the Software Collections packages.

The next-best option is to find whether the software author has packaged the version you want for your distribution. If they have, that's an easy answer, but a word of warning: The quality of the packaging varies enormously, and by 'packaging' I mean the installation and system management scripts that are bundled with the software to facilitate managing the software on your system. Ironically, in the case of commercial (paid-for) software, the general standard of packaging is considerably worse than the packaging done by the distributions or authors themselves.

A third option is to search the Internet to see whether someone has packaged the version you require for the distribution you are using, but the integrity of the software you download from an unknown source is itself unknown. Don't use this option.

It's possible to download the software source and compile it. This is often achievable without too much difficulty, but success is not guaranteed. Some knowledge of building software from source will certainly help, as will an understanding of the Linux development environment. It is likely that some – possibly many – supporting development packages will need to be installed to allow the software to be built. In general, we do not want to install any software on a production system that is not required for that system to fulfil its day-to-day function, and for this reason it is often better to compile and build the software elsewhere. Where possible, build it as a package to install on your system using the package manager (ie, for a Red Hat system build an RPM file), which allows the system to keep track of the installed files more easily. Ideally, add the resulting package to an internal package repository, which makes it much easier to manage package installations and updates across various systems.

Finally, you may want to install locally-written software. Similar considerations apply as for downloading the source, although one would hope that the software compilation will be more straightforward, and presumably there will be people who can help if it turns out not to be.

In all cases where you are installing software other than from the current version of your chosen distribution, consider how security updates will be handled. Certainly, if you build the package from source there will be no automated update or even notification of vulnerabilities, although many software projects have an 'announce' mailing list that will keep you informed (so subscribe to it). Other options may have some kind of security support; for example, the Debian backports repository implements security patches on a 'best efforts' basis – but there are no guarantees. In short, if you can avoid installing software that does not form part of the current release for your distribution, then do so.

OPERATING SYSTEM UPDATES AND UPGRADES

There are two kinds of periodic changes to the operating system itself, which we can distinguish with the terms *update* and *upgrade*.

The version number of any given Linux distribution release comprises a *major* and a *minor* number. For example, on 30 October 2018, Red Hat released version 7.6 of RHEL, which is major version 7, minor update 6. Changes to the minor version require an update; changes to the major version, an upgrade.

Updates will usually bundle together a number of changes:

- Low-priority security fixes

- Non-security bug fixes

- Packaging fixes

What won't be included are any major changes to the versions of installed packages. For example, in all versions of Debian 8, the PHP application shipped was version 5. There were different minor versions of PHP 5 during Debian 8's lifetime, but PHP 7 wasn't shipped until Debian 9.

Operating system updates – from one minor version to the next – are generally 'safe' to install, although it would be prudent to upgrade a development or test system first.

Operating system upgrades, where the major version number changes, should be treated as a separate project, and all business applications should be tested before rolling them out to production servers.

LONG-TERM SUPPORT

Some Linux distributions release new major versions very frequently; for example, Ubuntu has a new release every six months. That may be fine for an individual user's desktop, but upgrading servers or corporate desktops every six months would be a huge undertaking. The idea behind 'long-term support' (LTS) releases is that certain distribution releases are supported for a considerable length of time despite later, shorter-lifetime, releases. Again taking Ubuntu as an example, normal releases are made in April and October with each version being supported for nine months following release. The even-year April versions, though, are LTS versions, and are supported for five years from release. Not all distributions embrace the concept of specific LTS releases; Red Hat, for example, supports every major version of RHEL for at least ten years, although the level of support declines towards the end of that period.

The issue to be aware of with some LTS versions is that only a subset of the software packages have security updates released. This is a commonly misunderstood aspect of LTS releases. If you elect to use LTS releases, check with your distribution exactly what is included with LTS support. You may find that you are running a business-critical application that is not covered by the LTS security updates.

NOT INSTALLING UPDATES

Some organisations are very wary of security updates, possibly having been bitten in the past where a 'security' update did more than just fix a security problem and, in doing so, introduced other problems. It's certainly possible to introduce security updates in the same way as functional updates, via a testing phase before being rolled out to production, but be aware that that will incur a lot of overhead (a typical Linux server will receive multiple security updates each week). For many, choosing a distribution that is more disciplined with respect to only including security fixes in the updates, and possibly installing the updates twenty-four hours after they are released to allow any issues to surface, is a reasonable strategy. Some organisations take the view that the risk of issues arising from updates is greater than the risk of running software with known vulnerabilities. Think carefully before deciding upon that as your strategy.

SUMMARY

- Refer to security vulnerabilities by their CVE number rather than by the version of the software that purports to fix them

- Take care when installing software from sources other than your distribution repositories, particularly with regard to subsequent security updates

- If using an LTS distribution, ensure you understand which software packages are included in that support

Keeping systems up to date is a critical element of keeping them secure. This applies even to 'internal-only' systems, as discussed in Chapter 4. The vast majority of server compromises – ie, when servers are 'hacked' – are the result of those servers running software with known vulnerabilities and for which updates are available.

In short: ensure your monitoring system alerts you to any outstanding security updates, and have a process by which they are installed in a timely manner.

CHAPTER TWENTY

IT Projects

As we saw in Chapter 17, Request tickets are the mechanism by which we can track and implement small changes to the requirements of our Linux infrastructure – a new member of staff joins, a software package should be installed, and so on.

From time to time, larger changes are needed, and we can define them as 'Projects' rather than simple requests. It's worth considering what the scope of a Project might be, so here's a starting point:

- The provision of new services

- Planned downtime of a service of any duration during working hours

- Planned downtime of a service exceeding two hours at any time

- Work that will take more than one working day to complete

You will want to adapt this list to your own organisation.

IT projects have a notorious reputation for being late, being over-budget and not meeting expectations. This chapter is not about project management *per se*, but it is based upon the processes we use at Tiger Computing, which have helped us enormously. As well as reducing the time it takes us to implement projects, they've also made us more efficient and helped us 'get it right the first time'.

THE PROJECT REQUIREMENTS DOCUMENT

Some projects can appear deceptively simple, with 'obvious' requirements, but even simple projects often have more depth than may be initially realised, as the following example illustrates.

We sat in a room, just three of us, discussing the requirements of a client. They wanted to migrate their email from Google Mail to an in-house server, and had asked us if we could help. Their requirements were simple: build us a mail server.

Easy. What could possibly go wrong?

We just needed to know what domain the server should receive mail for. Or maybe 'domains'. Oh, and should users be able to access email only from within the company premises or from outside as well? Of course, we would need to consider the security policies for the mail server. And whether or not the client wanted to have shared mail folders. And if they did, who should have access to them? Is that read or write access? If someone reads a new mail in a shared folder, is it marked 'read' for everyone or just them? What about backups?

It seems quite a lot could go wrong.

Each of us in the room would have answers to most of those questions, but:

- Our answers may not be the same as each other's
- The client may have different answers still
- There may be other questions that we've not yet considered

At this point, the chances of success are slim. Even the definition of 'success' would be contested.

In the same way as our overall infrastructure has a Requirements Document, the starting point for a project should always be its Requirements Document. The goals of this document are to:

- Take into account the needs of the business

- Incorporate relevant experience

- Define what the end result is able to do

- Avoid mission creep

- Be complete, such that someone who has not previously worked on this project could implement it

- Be definitive

Importantly, a specific non-goal is to consider how the requirements will be met.

We'll explore each of those goals in a moment, but first let's consider who is going to write the Requirements Document. At first glance, the obvious author is 'the requester', but that's the wrong answer. Yes, they need input into the document, but the chances are that the IT Team or the IT Project Manager has more experience of implementing such projects. They know what questions need answering. There will often be previous experience that may be drawn on – the Requirements Document for the database server built last year could be a good starting point for this mail server.

From the requester's perspective, there may seem to be too many questions that need to be answered before work can begin, but those questions have to be answered at *some* point regardless. The truth is that it is much cheaper to answer them before we begin.

We're told repeatedly what the word 'assume' does, but there are times when making assumptions is a sensible thing to do. Writing the first draft of the Requirements Document is one such occasion. So long as we make it clear from the start that a) we have made lots of assumptions and b) we invite the requester to challenge or correct anything in the document, then we should be in a good place.

At this stage, do not define how the requirements will (or could) be met. This is one of the hardest traps to avoid. It's all too easy to couch the requirements such that they lead towards a (possibly unconsciously chosen) specific solution. Let's return to the Requirements Documents goals:

Take into account the requester's wishes: This is a given, of course; however, it's likely that the requester's expressed wishes will form a small part of the Requirements Document. Requesters are often surprised by the amount of detail that goes into that document (but very few question the amount of detail).

Incorporate relevant experience: The role of the IT Department should be to add value rather than just implement blindly. They will have seen it, done it, and may even have the T-shirt from prior Projects. They should also be familiar with industry best practices (which are not a constant). They will be aware of elements that the requester is less likely to think of that should be included in the Requirements Document, such as interoperation with other systems, security considerations and how the system will be backed up.

Define what the end result is able to do: This is the heart of the Requirements Document, and it is this that ensures everyone is rowing in the same direction.

Be complete: It's easy to leave inadvertent holes in the Requirements Document, but the proof that it's complete is when someone who has not previously worked on this Project can implement it. If they have to ask any questions ('When do you need this by?'), either they have not understood the Requirements Document fully or that document is deficient. This is where experience from previous Projects is invaluable: ensure that any questions that were asked last time are already answered in the Requirements Document.

Avoid mission creep: The bane of projects everywhere. 'If we're doing X, it would be very simple to do Y at the same time.' Well, if that's a requirement, document it in the Requirements Document.

If it's a suggestion, a thought, an idea, then add it to the list of 'Unanswered Questions' in the appendix to the Requirements Document – but all such questions must be answered prior to the start of implementation.

At Tiger Computing, we take a leaf from Fergus O'Connell's book, *Simply Brilliant*,[16] and answer the following questions at the start of the Requirements Document:

- How will we know when we're finished?
- What point in time constitutes the end point?
- What will the deliverables be?
- How will the quality of the deliverables be determined?
- What things are definitely part of this?
- What things are definitely not part of this?

During the development of the Requirements Document, anything at all may be changed. The end point is when all relevant parties agree that the Requirements Document is complete. There should be a formal acceptance that this version represents what the project is to deliver and that the Requirements Document is 'signed off' by both the requester and the project team.

---

16 O'Connell, F. (2004) *Simply Brilliant* (2nd ed.). Saddle River, NJ: Prentice Hall.

There is a second, optional, document that may follow the Requirements Document, and that is the Implementation Plan. In our experience, it's a helpful document, but not nearly so important as the Requirements Document. It also tends to be an internal document: the requester is often not interested in how it is done, only when it will be complete. The Implementation Plan may be little more than a list of actions and owners; for larger Projects, a more formal Project Plan may be needed.

Once the Requirements Document is complete, it is trivially easy to turn it into a checklist. For example, the requirement might be that the server will accept mail for the following domains:

- example.com
- example.co.uk

Mail for any other domain will be rejected.

We can turn this into a checklist:

☐ Server accepts mail for example.com

☐ Server accepts mail for example.co.uk

☐ Server rejects mail for server1.example.com

☐ Server rejects mail for example.net

Putting the Requirements Document together is hard work, but there shouldn't be any *wasted* work. If the requirements are not clearly defined in advance, then questions will arise during the implementation. Such questions interrupt the implementation process, they interrupt the requester, and they may delay the Project schedule. Incomplete requirements are also demoralising. Time set aside to implement something ideally ends with that something being implemented rather than waiting around for answers. In short, putting the hard work into the Requirements Document makes the implementation much easier.

Once complete, a post-Project review should be conducted. This is not an excuse to blame people for any mistakes that may have been made; rather, it's the means of ensuring that the next Project will be more successful. It's a good opportunity to improve the quality of the Requirements Documents over time. Here are a few questions worth asking:

- What did we do well?

- What did we do badly?

- What was missing from the Requirements Document?

- What's the one thing you would change in hindsight?

Here's how to ask them: gather all related parties together, and issue them with Post-It pads. As you ask the questions, each person should write any answers they have on separate Post-Its. When all questions have been asked, collect the Post-Its and group them by common concerns. A pattern will almost always emerge, and that's the feedback for the next Project. Finally, update your internal Project management process with the findings.

SUMMARY

- Write the Requirements Document first

- Avoid the word 'should' – this is requirements, not suggestions

- No implementation details

- No unanswered questions before the Project starts

- 'No blame' post-Project review findings must be written up

IT Project management is a complex subject in itself, and in this chapter we can only give an overview. However, for small- to medium-sized Projects, the guidelines above have proven their value over time and are worth adopting.

CHAPTER TWENTY ONE

Staff

Maintaining an IT infrastructure is hardly ever a one-person job. Unless your business *is* IT and you're the only person in the business, you'll need help. In this chapter, we look at what help is available, how you should go about finding it, and how to use it effectively.

The first decision is whether to support your infrastructure internally or outsource that support. Support is rarely 100% internal (you may need to hire specialists from time to time) or 100% external (someone will need to liaise with the support company). Be wary of trying an approach that's too hybrid; it's better if one entity manages the systems and infrastructure, albeit with guidance from other parties.

INTERNAL

The biggest advantage of directly employing IT staff is that you have complete control over what they do and when they do it. If you have something that you believe needs to be worked on right now, you can make that happen. That team is available to your business to use as you see fit.

There are, however, some challenges in directly employing IT staff:

- You're employing someone, with all the overheads that implies (salary and infrastructure costs, career development, people management, etc).

- You need more than one person. People take holidays, attend training courses and other external events, and occasionally become ill. If your business is reliant upon internal IT support staff, you need at least two.

- You need to attract good people. Good technical staff like a challenge and can quickly become bored in a static environment.

- You need technical oversight. Without that, it's not unusual to see home-grown, non-standard solutions implemented. Such solutions are often less effective and more expensive to support, particularly when the person who implemented them leaves the business.

- You need to retain them. If you're used to managing sales people (typically extroverted and highly motivated by money), you may find it challenging to recruit and retain good IT staff.

It's worth exploring that last point in more detail. In the same way that extroversion arguably makes a better sales person, the traits described below can be positive for IT staff. What follows is necessarily a generalisation, and of course there are talented IT specialists who don't conform to the stereotype described. However, over years of employing some of the best Linux technical staff available at Tiger Computing, this is what we've found.

Generally, in-depth technical staff tend to be more introverted than extroverted. They can be great team players but may prefer to work away from the centre of attention, focusing on getting the job done. They will often prefer the quieter end of the office and may opt to work from home more days per week than other team members. At the extreme, some are not overly comfortable on the telephone, so give them tools to support them through other communication channels, such as email, Instant Messenger or Slack.

They like to be in control of their environment. If you're expecting them to support Linux, don't insist that they use a Windows PC. If you tell them they can have whatever keyboard, mouse and monitor they want, they will be in awe. Don't bat an eyelid when they ask for a £100 keyboard – you'll get the value back many times over.

They know how they work best. Listening to music on headphones might strike you as distracting, but for many IT people it isn't. Multiple monitors are a plus. They hoard: at the back of the cupboard will be a memory stick of dubious provenance that 'might come in useful one day'. You can insist on a tidy-up once a year or so, but otherwise go with the flow.

They like solving problems and devising solutions. Don't tell them how to do their job; rather, tell them what results you want. Equally, don't ask them to implement a solution that you or someone else has devised; instead, tell them what problem needs to be solved. At the very least, involve them in the analysis of the problem and the design of the solution.

Regarding recognition: we all need money to live, but once they have a roof over their heads, food on the table and maybe a beer on Friday, their priorities change. Saying 'thank you' pays dividends (as it does for many staff). They will often value a technical training course more than the money it costs. For your best staff, give them a 'toys budget' of £1,000 or so that they can spend as they want on technical things without further approval.

You don't need to go to great lengths to treat IT staff differently from everyone else, but – as with all staff – it's worth recognising that different people work in different ways and have differing values. IT staff who are treated well, listened to, respected and given opportunities to grow will be very loyal.

One final point: developers can be very valuable staff members, and they may well be proficient at building and maintaining a development environment. However, they're seldom the best choice to manage a production environment. The requirements of each environment are different. The development environment is likely to be agile, flexible and possibly testing new technology, and focused on the immediate future. Conversely, the production environment needs stability and security, and needs to be part of a long-term coordinated plan.

OUTSOURCING

For most businesses, managing an IT infrastructure is not their core skill, and for that reason alone they often look to outsource that work to a business where that *is* the core skill. Some of the benefits of outsourcing include:

- Defined costs: So long as the deal is correctly structured, the costs will be known in advance and may be budgeted for. By 'correctly structured', I mean that the agreement should be to provide a level of service rather than a number of hours or Incidents.

- Access to expertise: Linux is a vast subject that includes which RAID system to use, how to configure highly-available clusters, which cloud infrastructure to use, which container system is right for you (if any), data encryption techniques – the list is huge. No one person has in-depth knowledge of all of it. Outsourcing to a business that designs, builds and maintains Linux systems every day of the week gives access to that expertise.

- Wide scope of experience: It's likely that what you are trying to do – or something very similar – has been done before. A good outsourcing partner will be able to bring experience of working with other clients to your situation, which will result in a quicker and more robust solution.

- Support infrastructure: A good, experienced specialist IT company will already have the components needed to manage an IT infrastructure, including systems for ticketing, monitoring, configuration management, backups, and so on.

- Proven processes: They will also have developed processes and methodologies to enable them to support their clients effectively and efficiently.

- Trained staff: In a business where IT is a core skill, it's likely that they will have invested in high-quality training for their staff.

- Up to date: Technology and the associated best practices evolve over time. A professional IT company will keep up to date with what's current and ensure that the solutions it manages are fit for purpose.

Most of all, though, for a company that provides outsourced Linux support, that's their core business. If they aren't good at doing that, they won't survive for long.

SUMMARY

- If you do employ IT staff, you need at least two people

- In-house IT staff, particularly in a small business, may lack the breadth of IT skills needed

- If IT isn't a core skill of your business, you may want to outsource the IT support

In this chapter, we've looked at two approaches to managing your Linux infrastructure. Employing staff directly has the advantage of direct control but brings with it the overhead of employing and managing people who may not have the breadth of skill that a specialist company can provide.

The alternative is to outsource the IT function to a specialist company. Choosing such a specialist company is a big enough subject to warrant a chapter of its own, so let's look at that now.

CHAPTER TWENTY TWO

Choosing An Outsource Partner

In the last chapter, we discussed the pros and cons of employing your own IT staff versus outsourcing that function. If you're looking for an outsource partner to design, implement or support your Linux systems, then by definition you're looking for a company that knows more about those things than you do – so how do you choose one? In this chapter, we look at seven areas you should discuss with any potential partner.

1. WHY THEM?

Start by asking them: 'Why should I choose to do business with you over any other option open to me?' If they cannot be crystal clear about why you should choose to do business with them, you can't be clear either.

It might sound simplistic, but answers such as, 'We provide excellent IT support, and our people are what make us different' aren't really answers at all. Just about every company will tell you that they are good and they have the best people.

2. HOW DO THEY HANDLE SECURITY?

When you delegate the support of your IT infra-structure to another company, you are handing over the keys to at least part of your business. Those who have keys to your house have built up trust with you, probably over a long period of time. Those who have the keys to your IT infrastructure need to earn that trust, too.

Security is a wide-ranging subject, as we've dis-cussed earlier, but here's a list of questions to ask that will at least give you some idea of how seriously a company takes security:

- How do you manage access to your customers' servers?

- How do you store passwords to your customers' systems?

- Who has access to those passwords?

- When do you use two-factor authentication?

- What is your process for keeping systems up to date with respect to security updates?

- How do you maintain an audit trail of work done?

- Are you accredited under ISO27001:2017, the current version of the Information Security Standard?

A good support contract will include the timely installation of security updates as they become available. It's important that your servers are kept up to date and secure, and this should be an integral part of the service, not a paid-for extra.

3. WHAT'S THEIR FOCUS?

When a company lists what it specialises in, be wary. 'Specialise' and 'lists', particularly long ones, don't sit well together.

If your business has chosen to run Linux servers, you want a support company that is serious about Linux. You don't expect your GP to be an expert on orthopaedic surgery; equally, you shouldn't expect an IT generalist to be able to provide the very best Linux support.

All IT companies will (presumably) fix things when they break, but that is not the same as keeping services available. You could ask:

- How quickly do you fix problems?

- Describe how you prevent problems occurring.

- How many support Incidents are included per month?

- If they monitor servers, ask:

  - Can I have access to that monitoring?

  - How many parameters are monitored on a typical server?

If you do have a problem, it must be easy to speak to someone who can actually help. Your time is too valuable to spend listening to dubious on-hold music.

4. HOW WILL THEY HELP REDUCE YOUR COSTS?

IT is not an end in itself but rather a means to an end. Your outsourced IT company should understand why your IT systems are in place and what they are there to achieve. If there is a better or cheaper way of achieving the same result, even if it involves fewer supported servers, they should tell you. Why would an IT support company tell you how to save money with them? Because they should be a partner, not simply an expense item.

5. WHAT QUALIFICATIONS DO THEIR STAFF HAVE?

Historically, there has sometimes been a gap in the IT industry between the technical qualifications held and the technical competence demonstrated. With that in mind, some Linux qualifications have been designed to be more rigorous.

The key qualifications in the Linux world (in no particular order) are:

- Red Hat Certified Engineer (RHCE): The exam requires the candidate to configure a (Red Hat) Linux system in various ways. This is a not a multiple-choice written test; it's a hands-on practical one. Verdict: a very high standard.

- Debian Developer (DD): This title is not achieved by passing an exam but by a peer-managed process of managing and maintaining Debian packages, and a deep understanding of the Debian philosophy. Verdict: a very high standard.

- Linux Professional Institute (LPI): Distribution-agnostic written exams administered by the non-profit Canadian Linux Professional Institute. There are many levels of certification. Verdict: a useful guide, but arguably not as deep as the RHCE and DD.

Be aware that qualifications lapse after a certain amount of time, so be sure to enquire about *current* qualifications.

6. CAN YOU VISIT THEIR OFFICES?

Most IT support companies won't have an issue with this, and it is a valuable thing to do. As discussed in question 2 ('How do they handle security?'), you're potentially handing over the keys to at least part of your business, so visiting their offices is a reasonable step in the process of due diligence.

If you do visit, what are you looking for? Here's a short list to get you started:

- Are they professional in their treatment of you and towards each other?

- How are they handling security with a stranger (you) in their midst?

- What's the office culture? What's on the desks and the walls? Would you want to work there?

- Are the answers given to your earlier questions reflected in what you see in the offices?

- Are the staff smart, professional and polite?

If their company website lists the IT support team, there's no harm in Googling them to see what kind of people they are.

7. WHAT DOES THE CONTRACT INCLUDE?

A professional IT support organisation will insist that both parties sign a contract. This isn't legal advice, but I believe the contract should include:

- Any minimum term and the required notice period. Neither should be excessive – you should be staying with them because you want to, not because you have to.

- The days and hours of cover.

- A confidentiality clause. They are likely to have full access to all your data, so this is essential.

- A Service Level Agreement: this defines the response you are entitled to for a given severity of problem – but be aware that 'response' is not the same as 'resolution'. This may also vary at different times of day.

What additional costs are not covered by the contract? Check for security updates, operating system upgrades, user requests, additions/changes/deletions to the services supported, and any limits on the number of Incidents.

You shouldn't expect to have to put the contract to test in a court, but having a contract ensures that both sides have a clear understanding of what will be provided at what cost.

SUMMARY

- Choose carefully: you're handing over the keys to your system

- Technical qualifications are valuable

- Certification, particularly to ISO27001:2017, is a good benchmark

A good outsource IT company can be a true business partner, able to help with not only the day-to-day support but also the other elements of building and managing a Linux solution as described in this book.

The seven areas discussed above will help identify those businesses with whom a partnership is most likely to be successful. If you end up with a shortlist of more than one, there are two final considerations that may help you choose:

- Do you like them? That may be unscientific, but you're unlikely to have a successful business relationship with people you don't like.

- Speak to their clients. Any respectable IT company will willingly provide references, and many people are more candid on the phone than in writing – so call a few. As well as their overall opinion, ask them what they wish they had known when they took out their support contract. Ask them about the service level, the professionalism, the partnership. How quickly is the phone answered? How quickly are problems resolved? What is their server availability like? Would they recommend their support company to others?

SECTION FOUR

EVALUATE

CHAPTER TWENTY THREE

Review Requirements

The process of designing, implementing and managing a Linux infrastructure starts with the requirements. The aim of the requirements is to define what is needed to meet the needs of the business. Over time, the requirements may change:

- The needs of the business may change.
  Businesses are not static, and a new product line, business growth or contraction, or a new market may dictate changes to the requirements.

- The existing requirements may not be correct. In the light of experience, it may become clear that too much (or not enough) focus has been put on one area, or maybe some requirements were omitted altogether through oversight.

- Technology changes. That *shouldn't* affect
  requirements – the technology is used to
  implement the requirements, not define
  them – but sometimes new technology causes
  us to think through the requirements in a
  different way. It's unlikely that Henry Ford
  included 'touchscreen navigation device' in his
  requirements for the Model T.

None of the above is unexpected. Businesses do
evolve, and the first cut of defining requirements
of an IT infrastructure is unlikely to be perfect. For
these reasons, the requirements should be reviewed
from time to time. There's one more reason to review
the requirements, and that is to ascertain whether
they have been fully implemented. It's not at all
uncommon for the actual infrastructure implementation to vary slightly from the requirements, but
such variance needs to be corrected, either in the
implementation or, if the requirements were incorrect, in the Requirements Document.

It's worth reviewing the Requirements Document
annually and with any major change to the business. Reviewing annually may feel like overkill, but
it's surprising how much things change in a year
without us being conscious that the requirements
are becoming outdated. The review should be a formal date in the calendar. It's easy to go for months
(years!) with 'Organise IT Requirements Review' on
the to-do list; get it in the calendar. If it turns out that

the requirements are in good shape, little time will be lost. If there are issues – well, you'll be glad you have a process to resolve them.

The output from the requirements review should be documented, and will typically consist of three sections:

- Amendments to the requirements

- A list of unmet (but valid) requirements

- Recommendations

HAVE REQUIREMENTS BEEN MET?

A good starting point is to check that the existing requirements are met. It should be easy to derive a checklist from the Requirements Document. Back in Chapter 4, we had a sample requirement:

Two-Factor Authentication is required for:

- Command line access to production servers
- Write access to the Company source code repository
- Edit access to the Company website

It's easy to put a checkbox next to each of the above points: Does command line access to production servers require 2FA? If so, tick and move on; if not, why not? Is the issue that it hasn't been implemented, or is the implementation faulty in some way? If it hasn't been implemented, is the requirement still valid as it stands, or should it be revised? Be wary of 'It's possible to get command line access at the system console without 2FA, but we know about that'. If it's not acceptable, list it as an unmet requirement. If it is acceptable, update the requirements.

NEW TECHNOLOGIES

For some people, new technology is seductive. 'Let's move everything to the cloud' is not an uncommon cry. 'We should adopt "bring your own devices (BYOD)"' and 'The tech staff love the new MacBook Pro, so let's give them one each'. Any or all of those may be valid suggestions, but a) none is a requirement (they are all implementations), and b) if they do stem from valid business requirements, those requirements should be reflected in the Requirements Document.

Let's consider cloud computing as an example. Many businesses have decreased their infrastructure costs, decreased the cost of ownership and increased resilience by migrating some or all of their infrastructure to cloud computing – but the fact that other businesses have done so does not *de facto* make it the right thing to do for yours. Cloud computing – like all technology – is a means to an end, and it should not be viewed as an end in itself. The driver has to be the business requirements. If there's a push for cloud computing, what is the business justification? If there's a perception that cloud computing may have a lower cost of ownership, an investigation can be added to the recommendations arising from the requirements review.

Similar arguments apply to other changes in technology. The mere availability of new technology does not automatically invalidate the current infrastructure. If the requirements haven't changed, older technology may be fine. The usual business justification for new technology is some kind of increase in efficiency coupled with a cost saving. The perception that such efficiencies are possible should lead to a fuller investigation in the first instance rather than a change of strategy.

The above may sound 'anti-cloud' or even Luddite, standing in the way of new technology. It's not. Huge sums of money are wasted every year by businesses jumping on the newest and shiniest bandwagon that passes or being seduced by the nice salesman from BigCo Ltd – or even just wanting to keep up with the Joneses. The process of insisting upon a written Requirements Document with a robust review process is intended to ensure that you have the most appropriate infrastructure *for your business*. In short, if you want to implement new technology, you should justify that change.

LOOKING AHEAD

We've confirmed that the existing requirements have been met, and we've considered any changes or recommendations we might want to make today. Finally, we need to look at the business plans for the next twenty-four months. What change do we expect to see in the business over that time? It may be more or bigger premises, more staff, new products, and so on. It may be that the business will be put up for sale or even contract in size. As best we can, we need to determine the IT infrastructure requirements of the business in twenty-four months' time, and carry out a gap analysis between where we are now and where we need to be then.

SUMMARY

The requirements review should:

- Confirm that the current infrastructure meets the requirements
- Accept that the requirements will evolve
- Be held regularly
- Confirm that the requirements are valid
- Confirm that the requirements are complete
- Confirm that the requirements are met
- Confirm that the requirements are fit for the next twelve to twenty-four months

CHAPTER TWENTY FOUR

Review Implementation

The implementation is intended to provide an environment that can meet the requirements. In many cases, any implementation deficiencies will become apparent in day-to-day operations. The requirements review may highlight some less obvious deficiencies in the implementation. In this chapter, we'll look at testing how well your infrastructure handles failures of various kinds. This chapter assumes that you have specified what the availability of data should be within your Requirements Document. Testing failures should be a regular item on your calendar – there's little point in spending time, money and effort mitigating the effect of hardware failure and human error only to find that when it does fail, so do the mitigations.

Sometimes it's helpful to consider how things might look after a failure. Here's what our (hypothetical) investigation into the failure found:

- The sole backups of the company's intellectual property were held on a single USB disk that was taken home by an employee each evening
- Restoring from backups had never been tested
- Recovering a system at a weekend relied on the goodwill (and availability) of staff to work on Sunday
- The Disaster Recovery documentation referred to systems that no longer existed

All of those 'findings' are taken from multiple actual examples, albeit not all of them have resulted in data loss for the organisations involved (yet). Can you imagine trying to find an appropriate answer when the boss, customer, shareholders, investors and/or press ask, 'Why were the backups never tested?'

It's tempting to put off testing, though. In the daily grind of business, with pressure to deliver the next project, to ship the next product, to keep customers (and shareholders) happy, testing how well your infrastructure responds to failure feels counterproductive. For this reason, such testing must have the buy-in from senior management. In the heat of the moment, getting a customer problem solved may feel more important than testing the backups. But in the cold loneliness of the night following data loss, you may concede that your priorities were misplaced.

Testing failure situations is as much a test of documented procedures as it is of actually recovering the data or service. Those procedures will be used for real very rarely, so it is important that they are tested thoroughly in advance.

There's another reason for having robust, tested processes in place: It's hard to think clearly and rationally under pressure. The reason airline pilots frequently test emergency situations in the simulator, such as an engine failure on take-off, is so that their reactions become automatic and correct. Once the immediate actions have been taken, they then rely on a checklist to ensure nothing is forgotten. They acknowledge that it's hard to think clearly and analytically in the heat of the moment, so they reserve the thinking for a time when the pressure is off, make a checklist, and use that when the pressure is on.

In our world, if a significant data restore needs to be carried out, there may well be a lot of pressure on those who are trying to restore that data. That is not the time to wonder how to access the backups, where to restore them to and in what order things should be done. Instead, they should be able to rely on the processes, procedures and checklists that were drawn up during calmer times. Once documented to the author's satisfaction, they should be tested by someone *other* than the author.

The correct approach to testing is to have a schedule. Each test should be documented along with the results, and the entire process must have the support of senior management. Here's an example schedule:

- February, August: test data restore

- May: test failure of server

- November: play out weekend disaster

That is by no means an extensive test schedule – there's nothing about penetration testing, for example – but implementing just what is listed here would be far more than most organisations do. Let's walk through each item in turn.

TEST DATA RESTORE

Testing a restore of data is by far the easiest test to undertake, and even in its simplest form it will either give some confidence that backup processes work or reveal some problems. Here's a minimal test that is easy to run. This isn't a rugged, comprehensive test of backups, but it is a good starting point. It's a five-day plan, and it will take less than two minutes a day.

Day 1: create a new document and store it wherever you would typically store documents. Don't call it 'My Backup Test' but rather something more realistic within your business. Put some text in this document. Mail a copy of it to your home email account.

Day 2: Open the document you created on day one and remove some (not all) of the text in it. Save it. Mail a copy of this version of the document to your home email account.

Day 3: Delete the document.

Day 4: Follow the normal process to get data restored (for example, raise a support ticket). Ask for the document you 'accidentally' deleted on day three to be restored. Upon completion, compare it with the copy you mailed home on day two.

Day 5: Request a restoration of the same document, but this time from the backup from day one. When complete, compare it with the copy you mailed home on day one.

There should be no reason why both copies of the document cannot be restored; if there is, you face potential data loss. It should be possible for the data restore to be carried out by a Level 1 member of the support team. When the restores are complete, ask the person who carried them out which process they followed. Check that the process is adequately documented and easy to follow.

TEST FAILURE OF SERVER

Testing how a failed server is recovered may be more invasive than a simple data restore, and thus the impact upon the business needs to be taken into consideration. The actual testing mechanism will depend upon the architecture of your infrastructure.

The easiest infrastructure to test is a cloud-based infrastructure. To test a server failure, simply shut down one running server instance, picked at random. There should be zero impact, and the 'failed' instance should be automatically replaced within a minute or two. Any other result indicates a lack of resilience.

With physical hardware, the server is either standalone or it is a component of a high-availability clustered system. In the latter case, failure simulation is easy: Physically disconnect all network connections to one server. The remaining systems should reconfigure as required to provide any services that the 'failed' server was providing. What we have simulated in this case is the complete loss of connectivity. More dramatic would be to simply pull the power lead(s) from the server, simulating a catastrophic failure of some kind. Whilst this is the most realistic, there is also a real risk of causing data corruption on the server. This risk is significantly lower than it was a few years ago, but it is still present. Disconnecting network connections is safer.

When reconnecting or powering up the 'failed' server – let's call it ServerF – your IT staff should carefully monitor the process. There is a potential problem in that ServerF's knowledge of the other systems may be outdated, which can lead to loss of data or data integrity. For example, ServerF and a second server – ServerX – may be configured as master/slave, and they may have data replicated from master to slave. Let's assume that ServerF is the master when it fails:

- Management software notices that ServerF has failed

- ServerX is promoted to 'master'

- Later, ServerF comes back online, but it still believes itself to be master

At this point, if both ServerX and ServerF believe they are master then it's likely that the data will not be correctly replicated between them. There are a variety of techniques to overcome this problem, but they are outside the scope of this discussion. What is important when ServerF is reconnected or powered up is that it re-joins its cluster gracefully.

In the case of standalone servers, deliberately disconnecting network or power connections will have an impact on the business. An alternative is to undertake a 'clean-room' build to simulate rebuilding the 'failed' server. Ideally, this will be carried out on standalone hardware to best represent the original environment, but often simply building a new virtual server will function as proof of concept that the 'failed' server can be rebuilt – or not. Your CMS can be used to build as faithful a replica of the production system as possible for these sorts of clean-room simulations.

The first time a server failure situation is to be tested, discuss it with your team. They will want the test to succeed, and they may have some good ideas about both how to test the failure scenario and whether the existing infrastructure is robust or not. However, at some point in the future, testing a failure scenario without prior warning would be prudent.

Testing backups deserves a discussion of its own. There's typically no need to restore all of the user data when testing a server rebuild of a data-rich server; it's possible (and valid) to test data restores in a different context. It may well be simpler to test restoring data to another server that has sufficient spare capacity.

There must be a feedback loop from the result of carrying out a restore back to the documented process, which will then evolve and mature over time. Some of the best people to test a restore process are newcomers, so when someone joins the IT team have them carry out a restore. Make it clear to them that it is the process, and not them, that is being tested.

Any questions they ask are highlighting deficiencies in the process.

Disaster Recovery plans should be reviewed frequently. You may be surprised at how much changes even within organisations that have a relatively static infrastructure: a different application is used, someone's contact details change, a service that was on a physical server has moved to the cloud, and so on. I recommend reviewing your Disaster Recovery plans at least quarterly. Better to have a frequent review with few changes than to find missing or incorrect data when it's most needed.

PLAY OUT WEEKEND DISASTER

Testing a full Disaster Recovery plan is a major undertaking. It will be very time consuming and will incur significant expense. For some organisations, such as airlines and banks, it will be necessary, but for many organisations it may not be viable to test a full disaster recovery scenario. If you choose not to carry out a full disaster recovery test, document that decision with your justification. You should, however, be able to demonstrate a full and complete recovery of your business-critical data without any access – physical or network – to your key place of business.

SUMMARY

- Test restores from backups

- Have a test schedule

- Discuss potential disaster scenarios with the IT team

In this chapter, we've looked at testing the resilience of your infrastructure in terms of recovery from failure, be that a system failure or a human shortcoming. Of course, we hope those things will never happen to us, but they *do* happen from time to time, and 'hope' is not a business strategy. Building in resilience is only the first part: we also have to test it. Perhaps most important of all is the feedback from the testing, which ensures that our infrastructure is ever more resilient.

CHAPTER TWENTY FIVE

Review Day-To-Day Operations

We've reviewed the requirements to ensure that they meet the needs of the business both today and tomorrow, and we've reviewed the implementation to ensure it meets the requirements. Finally, we need to review the day-to-day operations to ensure that they are fit for purpose.

It's easy to miss inefficient operations in a busy support department. Recurring but short-lived issues can be overlooked: the system backup that fails once or twice a month but is fine the rest of the time, the idiosyncrasies of a software tool that users work around without really thinking about it, and so on. For those reasons, it's worth reviewing operations more frequently than the requirements and infrastructure, and every three months is a good starting point.

There will be statistics available – the number of tickets closed per week, the average time to resolve an Incident, system availability, and so on – but often a better starting point is gut feel. Is the day-to-day IT support essentially working or is it broken?

PROCESSES

At its most basic level, operations comes down to the implementation of processes. If support operations are breaking on a day-to-day basis then either the processes aren't being followed or they are broken. The former is exposing either a training issue (the staff don't know that there is a process or they don't know how to follow it) or a disciplinary issue (they do know about the process and how to follow it, but they haven't done so). If a process is broken, it will be for one of the following reasons:

The process doesn't exist: Of course, if a process doesn't exist then it can't be followed, but it's worth examining *why* it doesn't exist. It could be simple oversight, but more often the reason is subtler. Perhaps circumstances have changed – maybe a new software tool has been introduced – or something has happened that wasn't foreseen. As well as correcting the situation by writing the new process, it is worth examining whether anything could have indicated the need for a new process earlier.

The process is ambiguous: It is hard – sometimes very hard – to write a process that is complete, accurate and easy to follow. When initially writing a process, have someone else who has been uninvolved in writing it test it. Even that won't reveal all of the process's problems, and it's possible that someone follows a process in good faith but still doesn't do what was intended. This is *not* a training issue: it is process problem. One tip that may help: keep processes tight, with the minimum number of steps needed, and make each step a short statement. If you're using a wiki to document your processes, make liberal use of links. One step might be 'Log into the backup system', which itself might be a link to a more detailed page explaining how to do that. For the person familiar with the backup system, the five words in that step tell them all they need to know, and they keep the process focused. For those less familiar with the backup system, the information is easily available but doesn't clutter up the process.

The process is impractical: Clues that a process may be heading this way include:

- A requirement for more than one person in order to complete the process
- A process that takes more than half a day to run

- Process documentation that takes up more than a screenful of text

- Too many 'if's in the process

- A process that tries to achieve more than one thing

The solution is to simplify, rewrite or split into multiple processes. Again, have someone who has not been previously involved test the process. If they have any questions or hesitation, your process is still broken.

Processes evolve. They change not only because the environment changes but also in the light of experience. Knowing where more detail is required, knowing when to link to another page, knowing when to split or combine processes – all that comes with experience. The operations review is part of that experience.

TRENDING TICKETS

A spate of similar tickets might be spotted by the support staff, but, even if it is, there's no guarantee that they'll take specific action in light of the trend. Consider the example of a server backup failing two to three times a month. The most likely reaction is, 'Oh, it does that from time to time. See if it runs OK tonight.' The first time round, that might – only *might* – be an appropriate response, but after a few weeks of irregular backup failures a more proactive approach is called for.

One agenda item on the quarterly operations review should be a review of trending tickets. Somewhat unscientifically, just looking at the list of tickets created since the last review can reveal patterns. Sorting the tickets in some appropriate way can help, perhaps by system, department or, where appropriate, client.

The correct reaction to repeated similar tickets is to create a Problem ticket and take a closer look. Recall from Chapter 17 that a Problem ticket covers a 'condition often identified as a result of multiple incidents that exhibit common symptoms'. There is a reason why the backups fail on Server X every ten to fourteen days, and whilst resolving that issue may not be urgent, it's certainly important.

TEAM SKILLS

If you have a team of IT support staff, you will want to ensure that all areas of technology that you use are covered by more than one of them. The clues to look out for are always assigning a given type of problem to the same person – if Kate always deals with network routing issues, what will you do when she's not available? Even when multiple people are trained in one area, it can still be that tickets about that area gravitate towards one person. Don't let them. Ensure that such tickets are deliberately given to the trained but less experienced person: it is much better that they gain the experience whilst Kate is available to help if required.

At Tiger Computing, we have a 'Technical Training Checklist' page on our internal wiki, which lists all the technical skills needed to be able to support our clients. That page is used to tailor a per-person technical training plan for each support consultant. The list itself is reviewed regularly to ensure that all skills listed are relevant and that it's up to date. There's a second page, 'Out-of-Hours Knowledge', which lists the skills the technical staff must be competent at before they may participate in the out-of-hours rota. That list too is reviewed regularly.

TOOLS

Finally, it's worth reviewing the tools you use to manage the day-to-day operations. They will probably include, amongst other things:

- A ticketing system

- A CMS

- A wiki

- A monitoring system

- An online chat application

- A version control system

- A time tracking or reporting tool

Your review should cover how the tools are used and how fit for purpose they are. Some examples of issues you may encounter:

- Too many wiki pages were out of date. Despite encouraging users to update inaccurate pages as they discovered them, it wasn't happening. A system was introduced whereby pages could, with one click, be tagged as needing revision. A 'wiki sprint' day was organised when everyone worked on updating the tagged pages.

- The monitoring system had some usability issues, particularly around configuration, which meant that certain critical applications on servers weren't always being monitored. A project was undertaken to see whether those usability issues could be resolved, but the ultimate conclusion was that a different monitoring system would be more suited to the organisation as it grew.

Changing tools is disruptive and painful, and will thus not be undertaken lightly. However, as in the second example above, sometimes it's the right thing to do. There comes a time when the persistent pain of staying with the incumbent is greater than the (hopefully) short, sharp pain of changing.

SUMMARY

- Keep processes tight

- Review trending tickets

- Ensure technical skills are distributed amongst your staff

In this chapter, we've looked at how a review of the day-to-day operations may be carried out. Reviewing the operations is not as clear-cut as reviewing, say, the requirements. It requires that we actually open our eyes and look for problems; operations, being a human activity, often includes pain that is just tolerated because 'that's how it is'. Sometimes, simply asking staff, 'What one thing would you change to make your day-to-day life better?' may reveal the pearl of wisdom you seek.

Golden Rules

- Test backups.

- Actively decide *not* to do things rather than just putting them off.

- Don't receive reports that are routinely ignored.

- Don't ignore reported errors.

- Use independent checks.

- Use checklists.

- Keep documentation up to date.

- Everything starts with requirements.

- Routinely evaluate requirements, implementation and support.

- Test backups. Again.

Acknowledgements

I imagine that most people who read the acknowledgements section in books are looking for a name they recognise (preferably their own). There's an element of the awards speech too: a long list of people to thank. There's usually some comment about how the book wouldn't have been possible without them, and how it's impossible to name them all.

It's all true.

This book is about Linux, about business, about technology, but more than anything it's about how to *think* about Linux solutions. It took me a long time to acknowledge that not everyone thinks about things the way I do. It took me even longer to learn that sometimes there was a better way. To those who took on the task of persuading me of those facts: thank you. I believe it was worth it. I hope your scars heal.

My parents, Jenny and Derek, deserve thanks for millions of things, but teaching me that I am responsible for my destiny ranks high. So does buying me that Meccano set. Thank you.

For believing in my business, thank you Mark Lewis, our first ever customer. That changed Tiger Computing from a nice idea into something real. All of our clients over the years have helped shape and refine our business, what we do and how we approach it. Many of you I regard as more than 'just clients'. Thank you, too.

The team, past and present, at Tiger Computing, including Ben, Chris, Jonathan, Nye and Rick: you are amazing people to work with, and have inspired much of what lies within these pages.

There are a number of people who fall into the category of 'When they speak, I listen'. Amongst them are Nigel Botterill (for telling me straight, and for pointing out the most significant line in the film *Apollo 13*) and Daniel Priestley (without whom this book probably wouldn't exist). Thank you for speaking whilst I was listening.

And then there is a remarkable group of business colleagues that I'm privileged to regard as friends. The impact you have on me, my business and my life is profound. Thanks Glenn, David, Neil, Steve, Pieter, Felicity and Alan. No surnames needed: you know who you are.

To Lucy, my daughter: what an amazing person you are. Smart, funny, thoughtful and caring (your mother's genes clearly won that battle). Even though you are 'only' 12, I've learned from you. Thank you for being the best PuddleDuck in the whole wide world.

And then there's Cecilia, my wife. Without you, none of this makes sense. You understand me (how?), support me and are simply there. You make me a better person. How could I ever ask for more? Thank you.

PS – This was the hardest page to write. I'm blaming the onions.

The Author

Keith Edmunds is an award-winning entrepreneur who has worked in the IT industry since 1980. Initially working with hardware, he quickly moved to a consultancy role helping businesses make the most of their IT investment. He's worked with companies such as Citibank, Unilever, Birds Eye Walls and Ericsson, as well as leading bioscience research companies.

Excited and intrigued by Linux, he followed its development throughout the 1990s, using it within the workplace from time to time. By the end of that decade, it became apparent that Linux had much to offer businesses. Quite apart from the zero-cost licence, he felt the Open Source philosophy would also be good for businesses. He set about researching how to help businesses make the most of Linux, and Tiger Computing was the result.

Today, Keith is still a keen Linux advocate, but he takes the view that, for most businesses, Linux is merely a means to an end. The starting point has to be the business requirements, not the technical solution.

Outside of work, Keith plays with guitars, aeroplanes, gliders (he's a qualified gliding instructor) and his twelve-going-on-sixteen-year-old daughter. One takes far more time than all the others combined.

Contact details

keith@tiger-computing.co.uk

www.linkedin.com/in/keith-edmunds

@tigercomputing

www.tiger-computing.co.uk